1993

High School–College Partnerships:
Conceptual Models, Programs, and Issues

by Arthur Richard Greenberg

ASHE-ERIC Higher Education Report No. 5, 1991

Prepared by

Clearinghouse on Higher Education
The George Washington University

In cooperation with

Association for the Study
of Higher Education

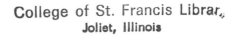
Published by

School of Education and Human Development
The George Washington University

Jonathan D. Fife, Series Editor

Cite as

Greenberg, Arthur Richard. 1991. *High School-College Part-
nerships: Conceptual Models, Programs, and Issues.* ASHE-ERIC
Higher Education Report No. 5. Washington, D.C.: The George
Washington University, School of Education and Human
Development.

Library of Congress Catalog Card Number 92-80181
ISSN 0884-0040
ISBN 1-878380-10-9

Managing Editor: Bryan Hollister
Manuscript Editor: Alexandra Rockey
Cover design by Michael David Brown, Rockville, Maryland

The ERIC Clearinghouse on Higher Education invites individuals to submit proposals for writing monographs for the
ASHE-ERIC Higher Education Report series. Proposals must
include:
1. A detailed manuscript proposal of not more than five pages.
2. A chapter-by-chapter outline.
3. A 75-word summary to be used by several review committees for the initial screening and rating of each proposal.
4. A vita and a writing sample.

ERIC Clearinghouse on Higher Education
School of Education and Human Development
The George Washington University
One Dupont Circle, Suite 630
Washington, DC 20036-1183

This publication was prepared partially with funding from
the Office of Educational Research and Improvement, U.S.
Department of Education, under contract no. ED RI-88-062014.
The opinions expressed in this report do not necessarily
reflect the positions or policies of OERI or the Department.

EXECUTIVE SUMMARY

Awareness of high school-college partnerships has increased, especially in the higher education community, as evidenced by increased numbers of partnerships, legislative activity, publications, news reports, foundation and agency support, and conferences and panels devoted to the subject. While the roots of the (often strained) relationships between high schools and colleges go back two centuries or more, the closer collaboration required for successful partnerships is a relatively recent phenomenon.

What Accounts for the Interest In High School-College Partnerships?

Many factors explain the burgeoning interest in collaboration including the changing student population, democratization of higher education admissions policies, students' frequent lack of skills preparedness, awareness of a need for new models of inservice staff development for high school teachers, and greater competition in college student recruitment. Additional factors include increased awareness of the need for enhanced articulation between levels of institutions by administrators, parents, and state education department officials, and an awareness that the challenges confronting contemporary secondary education—particularly for at-risk students, women, and minorities—require a community effort in which colleges have been asked to play a much larger role than previously reserved for them.

In the face of increased opportunities to consummate partnerships with school systems, higher education institutional decision makers must respond to several key questions including: What are our institutional motives? Can our expertise be transferred to elementary and secondary school settings? Which partnership form is the correct form for us? Is this an opportunistic involvement created by external pressures or inducements (such as grant opportunities), or are we seeking a longer term relationship with requisite resources identified to sustain the effort? Is the partnership consistent with our perceived institutional mission? Can our institution afford to risk failure?

Can High School-College Differences Be Overcome?

The movement toward partnerships has not been without its natural impediments. Practitioners and researchers have commented upon the differences in high school and college

146,677

cultures. These differences have evolved from disparities in institutional funding and resources, student bodies, teachers and teaching (including teaching load, student characteristics, source and availability of materials of instruction, academic freedom, salaries and vacations, teaching amenities, teaching qualifications, valuing performance, and rewards), faculty role in decision making, and institutional leadership style. These factors, combined with the historical separateness of our loosely coupled systems of secondary and postsecondary education, have led in their most benign form to a lack of mutual understanding. More invidious manifestations can result in an active distrust between high school and college faculty and administrators.

Fortunately, a growing body of collaborative experience demonstrates that these factors can be overcome with appropriate planning and sensitivity to divergent, as well as congruent, institutional goals and cultures.

What Forms Do Partnerships Take?

Examples of high school-college partnerships include concurrent-enrollment models; enrichment, compensatory, and motivational designs; Academic Alliances and other teacher-to-teacher approaches; preservice teacher education; mentoring/tutoring models; and school improvement and restructuring efforts.

Concurrent-enrollment models provide an opportunity for high school students to engage in college-level courses, usually for simultaneous high school and college credit. Examples of the model include the College Board's Advanced Placement Program and Syracuse University's Project Advance, both designed to serve students who show well-above-average academic ability; La Guardia Community College's Middle College High School, for students at risk; Minnesota's Post-secondary Enrollment Options Program, for students of all ability levels; and Virginia's Master Technician Program for technical students.

Other partnerships focus on enrichment, compensatory, and motivational concerns, often for students who are at risk (urban and rural poor, for example), underrepresented (women in science and minority group members), or traditionally not well served through conventional programs (such as gifted or talented students). Programs representative of these types include the University of California's MESA,

Colorado Community College's Partners Program, and the Center for the Advancement of Academically Talented Youth at Johns Hopkins University.

Academic Alliances and other kinds of teacher-to-teacher partnerships, through which high school and college faculty jointly discuss a variety of subject-area issues and concerns, also prevail. The Greater Boston Foreign Language Collaborative is an excellent example of the Academic Alliance movement. The National Writing Project, the Atlanta Public Schools project with the National Faculty, and the Yale-New Haven Teachers Institute are other examples of teacher-to-teacher partnerships.

Other partnerships have developed in the areas of pre-service teacher education (such as Cleveland State University's teacher training centers); student mentoring/tutoring programs (for example, the University of Akron's Kenmore Project); and partnerships which have as their objective school improvement or restructuring (Mississippi's Project '95 and the College Board's EQ Models Program for School-College Collaboration).

What Issues and Actions Should an Institution Consider When Contemplating Involvement In Partnerships with High Schools?

Five steps are key to the development of any high school-college partnership:

- Identify the student population and program goals
- Contact local high schools and school districts
- Determine costs
- Develop community support
- Evaluate for program improvement

Because the field of high school-college partnerships still is actively developing, significant research issues remain to be addressed. These issues tend to fall into three major areas: descriptive, procedural analysis, and outcomes analysis.

Unless a sound sense of the realistic anticipated outcomes of high school-college partnerships can be established, their future viability cannot be assured; nor, perhaps, can they even appropriately be justified apart from the accounts of their many supporters.

ADVISORY BOARD

Alberto Calbrera
Arizona State University

Carol Everly Floyd
Board of Regents of the Regency Universities System
State of Illinois

L. Jackson Newell
University of Utah

Barbara Taylor
Association of Governing Boards of Universities and Colleges

J. Fredericks Volkwein
State University of New York–Albany

Bobby Wright
Pennsylvania State University

CONSULTING EDITORS

Paula Y. Bagasao
University of California System

William E. Becker
Indiana University

Rose R. Bell
New School for Social Research

Louis W. Bender
Florida State University

David G. Brown
University of North Carolina–Asheville

David W. Chapman
State University of New York–Albany

Linda Clement
University of Maryland

James Cooper
FIPSE College Teaching Project

Richard A. Couto
Tennessee State University

Donald F. Dansereau
Texas Christian University

Peter Frederick
Wabash College

Mildred Garcia
Montclair State College

Virginia N. Gordon
Ohio State University

Wesley R. Habley
American College Testing

Dianne Horgan
Memphis State University

Don Hossler
Indiana University

John L. Howarth
Private Consultant

William Ihlanfeldt
Northwestern University

Susan Jeffords
University of Washington

Greg Johnson
Harvard College

Margaret C. King
Schenectady County Community College

Joseph Lowman
University of North Carolina

Jean MacGregor
Evergreen State College

Christine Maitland
National Education Association

Richard Morrill
Centre College

Laura I. Rendón
North Carolina State University

R. Eugene Rice
Antioch University

Richard Robbins
State University of New York–Plattsburg

Carol F. Stoel
American Association for Higher Education

Susan Stroud
Brown University

Stuart Suss
City University of New York–Kingsborough

Marilla D. Svinicki
University of Texas–Austin

Elizabeth Watson
California State University–Humboldt

Janice Weinman
The College Board

William R. Whipple
University of Maine

Roger B. Winston
University of Georgia

REVIEW PANEL

Charles Adams
University of Massachusetts–Amherst

Richard Alfred
University of Michigan

Philip G. Altbach
State University of New York–Buffalo

Louis C. Attinasi, Jr.
University of Houston

Ann E. Austin
Vanderbilt University

Robert J. Barak
Iowa State Board of Regents

Alan Bayer
Virginia Polytechnic Institute and State University

John P. Bean
Indiana University

Louis W. Bender
Florida State University

Carol Bland
University of Minnesota

Deane G. Bornheimer
New York University

John A. Centra
Syracuse University

Arthur W. Chickering
George Mason University

Jay L. Chronister
University of Virginia

Mary Jo Clark
San Juan Community College

Shirley M. Clark
Oregon State System of Higher Education

Darrel A. Clowes
Virginia Polytechnic Institute and State University

CONTENTS

FOREWORD

It is not particularly noteworthy that Charles Robb, Democratic senator from Virginia, and William Bennett, Republican and former secretary of education, have both supported the concept that if higher education institutions raised their admission qualifications, high schools automatically would raise their standard of education. What is noteworthy is that they both intuitively recognized the importance of the interrelationship between colleges and high schools. Quite simply stated, quality of collegiate education is influenced by the quality of high school education and vice versa. The future of each is dependent on the performance of the other.

This interrelationship is not new; it just has been ignored. The United States did not have universal higher education until the turn of the century. Up until this time, higher education institutions played a major role in nurturing curriculum development in and setting standards for high school education. During his tenure as president of the University of Michigan (1852-1863), Henry Tappan worked with the Michigan public schools to establish mutually agreeable academic standards. In doing so, he set a precedent for future partnerships between higher education and public high schools. Somehow, the strength of this link between colleges and high schools has dwindled since the 1920s.

One obvious interrelationship between colleges and high schools lies in teacher training. Most schools of education— if not all—have some sort of practicum or clinical experience that places their students in a classroom. However, the schools don't take advantage of the practicum to update faculty on the actual issues affecting their subject—ie. high school teaching—as, for example, do medical faculty at their teaching hospitals. Few, if any, schools of education mandate that their faculty spend a minimum amount of time in actual practice.

Less obvious, but equally important: An interdependent relationship involves all the academic areas of undergraduate education. If, as is so often reported, the quality of undergraduate education is significantly limited because entering students are poorly prepared, then it would seem logical that the faculty in these areas would work directly with the institutions responsible for developing these students. It is ironic that higher education institutions don't plant the seeds for the high quality students they desire!

In this monograph, Arthur Richard Greenberg, superintendent of Schools at Community School District 25 in

Queens, N.Y., and former dean for freshman skills at LaGuardia Community College, City University of New York, begins with an overview and history of high school-college partnerships. He gives significant attention to the cultural discontinuity that exists between high school and college cultures and to the differences in institutional funding and resources, student bodies, teachers and teaching, faculty roles in decision making and institutional leadership styles. The report highlights several models actually in use, including concurrent-enrollment models; enrichment, compensatory, and motivational designs; Academic Alliances and other teacher-to-teacher approaches; preservice teacher education; mentoring/tutoring models; and school improvement and restructuring efforts.

Colleges and high schools do not exist separately; they are interdependent. If this interdependence is recognized and nurtured, a powerful synergy can develop. If this interdependence is ignored, both areas suffer. Colleges need to establish within their academic culture the legitimacy of developing closer academic ties with high schools. Conversely, high schools need to be less defensive as they work out partnership arrangements with colleges. These partnerships are not only desirable, they are necessary. For those who recognize this need and those who work to refine the partnerships of the future, Dr. Greenberg's report is greatly useful.

Jonathan D. Fife
Series Editor, Professor, and
Director, ERIC Clearinghouse on Higher Education

ACKNOWLEDGMENTS

I wish to acknowledge the assistance I received from and the patience shown me by my wife Fran, my daughter Jessica, and my son Jonathan during the time I took from them in order to work on this project.

To them I am always grateful, and it is to them that this work is dedicated.

HIGH SCHOOL-COLLEGE PARTNERSHIPS
GAIN INCREASING ACCEPTANCE:
A View of Contemporary Educational and Political Forces at Play

Evidence of High School-College Partnership Interest

A cursory look at today's education scene evokes the correct sense that high school-college partnerships are a topic of major interest. Indeed, this monograph was developed as the result of an ASHE-ERIC poll of college administrators who were asked to denote pressing areas of concern.

Interest in these partnerships is ascending in higher education circles. Factors such as increasing numbers and sizes of existing partnerships, pertinent action by state legislatures, new foundation support for partnership replication efforts, and secondary and postsecondary school-reform efforts all have helped to place high school-college partnerships on the "action list."

The recent growth of partnership forms—and the creation of new ones—has been well documented. This monograph focuses on several forms, including concurrent-enrollment models, compensatory education models, Academic Alliances, and preservice teacher education, among others. One of the oldest partnership programs, the College Board's Advanced Placement Program, has increased in size to the point at which nearly 300,000 students take about 425,000 AP examinations annually (College Board 1989), representing a threefold increase over the previous decade (Number of Students 1985).

Syracuse University's Project Advance and the College Now programs, both concurrent-enrollment programs, have increased the numbers of sites at which their programs are offered as well as the number of student participants (Wilbur 1984; Greenberg 1987). The same may be said of Minnesota's Educational Options program (Berman 1985; Randall 1986). The number of school districts and college faculty who participate in educational alliances steadily has increased (Gross 1988; Bagasao 1990).

Legislative actions also indicate an increased interest in partnerships. Several states, perhaps most notably Minnesota and Florida, require colleges and local school districts to negotiate concurrent-enrollment plans, allowing high school students to take college courses without tuition expense (Florida Administrative Code 1983; Randall 1986). Other states specifically have funded high school-college partnership efforts. For example, New York State has funded College Now, Middle Colleges, and mentoring efforts, as well as the $30 million

Legislative actions also indicate an increased interest in partnerships.

Liberty Partnerships Program (College Option 1985). In California, CAPP (California Academic Partnerships Program) has focused the attention of high school-college teams at 19 sites on improving the academic preparation of junior and senior high school students. Money allocated by the state legislature supports this effort ("Mainstreaming" 1990).

A very short list of the many foundations, both large and small, local and national, which have supported investigation in the field of high school-college partnerships includes the following: the Ford Foundation, which has supported evaluation and replication of the Middle College model design through technical support and conferences (Lieberman 1986); the MacArthur Foundation, for its support of the work of the Educational Alliance movement in which Claire Gaudiani has been a key player and advocate (Gaudiani and Burnett 1986; Vivian 1985a; Ascher 1988); the Diamond Foundation, which has supported the work of community college exploration in the field of teacher preparation; and various Carnegie-affiliated groups that have supported conferences and publications dealing solely or in part with the topic (Carnegie Council 1979; Carnegie Forum 1986).

The school reform movement has considered the potential significance of high school-college partnerships. The following commentators and organizations have remarked on the need to restructure high school-college relationships as a route toward school reform: Ernest L. Boyer (1983, 1987), John Goodlad (1988, 1989), and the National Association of Secondary School Principals (AAHE et al. 1986).

From the publishing field also comes ample additional evidence that the new focus on high school-college partnerships is widespread. A recent computer search using the phrase "college school cooperation" of articles in periodicals in the ERIC system since 1976 using the phrase "college-school cooperation" of periodical articles in the ERIC system since 1976 produced more than 1,000 references. The number of recent publications focusing on high school-college partnerships far exceeds the space limitations of this section for their full citation. Suffice to say, however, that the field has been the concern of scholars, educational reformers, theorists, researchers, and journalists, and many of their works will be cited throughout this monograph.

Professional groups, foundations, and agencies concerned with both the secondary and postsecondary levels also have made partnerships a frequent subject for conferences. Significant related events during the last decade might include a meeting in 1983 of chief state school officers and college university presidents titled "School and College Partnerships in Education," sponsored by the Carnegie Foundation for the Advancement of Teaching (Watkins 1983), and a conference, "The School-College Connection," jointly sponsored in 1984 by the National Association of Secondary School Principals, ACE, and the American Association of Collegiate Registrars and Admissions Officers (Thomson 1984).

One also might wish to include the conference "School-College Partnerships: The State of the Art," held in 1985 in Minneapolis and sponsored by FIPSE, the Academic Skills Project of the University of North Dakota, AAHE, and the Council of Chief State School Officers (The School-College Partnerships 1985). In June 1990, a new annual event was created, jointly hosted by the AAHE and The College Board. Called the Conference on School/College Collaboration, it was held in cooperation with the National Association of Secondary School Principals, the Education Commission of the States, and the Council of Chief State School Officers (Albert 1990).

Virtually all other major secondary and postsecondary associations have sponsored individual sessions on the topic at their national and regional conferences.

Partnerships: Why Now?

As with so many policy issues, the heightened interest in high school-college partnerships cannot be traced to a single trend, event, individual, group, or institution. Rather, the confluence of several of these factors over time has resulted in the current interest in these partnerships. Several issues—all in some way tied to school reform efforts—are seminal to the current spurt in partnership growth and therefore worthy of discussion.

Carnegie raises issues old and new

In 1967, the Carnegie Foundation for the Advancement of Teaching founded the Carnegie Commission on Higher Education. The work of these two bodies as well as the work of related organizations has raised concerns about and changed the nature of the high school-college partnership debate and the school reform movement over the upcoming two decades. The commission's reports in 1971 and 1973 provided a new focus on some longstanding issues such as the discontinuities among all levels of education as well as some new issues: curriculum redundancy and significant changes in the secondary and postsecondary populations.

Curriculum redundancy. The issue of curriculum redundancy or duplication was not unknown prior to the Carnegie Commission reports. It had, however, only occasionally become a point of contention as both secondary and postsecondary educators found it in the interests of their respective preserves to address curriculum concerns autonomously. Each group resisted mightily outside attempts to prescribe the elements of a standard education. Both felt that whenever possible these were decisions that were better left to institutional-level decision making.

Yet the research shows that left to their own devices, secondary and postsecondary institutions often develop curricula that overlap, especially for the last two years of high school and the first two years of college (Carnegie Commission 1973; Casserly 1965; Snyder 1974). While some repetition might be desirable, especially for students who have basic-skills deficits, research shows that curricular redundancy seems to occur more often for students of superior ability than for students with poorer academic records (Eurich and Stanton 1960).

Several researchers have examined the extent of duplication in high school and college study. One of the earliest to investigate this area was Osborn, who found that between 17 percent and 23 percent of high school English, history, and physics topics were repeated in college (1928). "General Education in School and College," a comprehensive study of the curricula of six high schools and six colleges, revealed "questionable duplication, wasted time, and damage to student interest and academic motivation" in history, literature, and especially in the sciences (1952, p. 7).

Enrollment data and tuition costs indicate that $420 million were spent in 1965 to teach courses in colleges that already had been taught in high schools (Blanchard 1971). Observing the increases in the Consumer Price Index over the last quarter century, this translates into more than $1.5 billion today (Statistical Abstract 1986).

Changing student population. The changing student body also has been a key ingredient in the recent debates. The regents of the University of New York in 1974 stated: "Many young people are physically, socially, and intellectually more advanced today than their parents were at the same age."

With new concerns about educating a more mature and intellectually advanced student body, points of curricular redundancy rife in the air, and the more than century-old issue of the discontinuity between high schools and colleges about to come once again into the public arena, articulation became an issue whose moment had arrived.

Recent trends in school-college articulation

Factors fueling school reform debate. It is perhaps not coincidental that debate over high school-college relationships should take place in an era of renewed scrutiny of the U.S. system of education. Additional factors that were involved in creating an active audience for the debate included declining college enrollments (Breland 1986; Two-Year Colleges 1986), increasing college tuition costs, public reluctance to support increased secondary school spending (Hymes 1981), a general teacher shortage (Carnegie Forum on Education and the Economy 1986), and an acute minority teacher shortage (Quality Education for Minorities Project 1990). A series of reports—in particular, *A Nation at Risk* (National Commission on Excellence in Education 1983)—heightened public perception of the crisis in our schools.

Concomitant has been the theme of concern for minority access and equity in secondary and postsecondary education. This concern has been reflected in a number of major reports and projects including *School/College Collaboration: Teaching At-Risk Youth* (Yount and Magrun 1989) and the Carnegie Corporation-supported Quality Education for Minorities Project (1990).

High school-college partnerships: a recurring reform theme. The wideranging set of public secondary and postsecondary education afflictions commonly cited includes lack of public support, budget crises, staggering dropout rates, limited minority retention and graduation rates, an aging faculty, an extremely limited pool of potential teachers from minority groups, few minority doctorates being produced (and still fewer in mathematics and hard sciences), the relative absence of teachers' voices in decisions affecting their professional lives, the changing demographics of the public school student body, and the concern about redundancy between high school and college instruction. What begins to emerge from the various viewpoints about these problems is a common perception that high school-college partnerships, combined with other strategies, can play significant and varied roles in solving these problems.

In light of this surging trend, one might query why it has taken so long for high schools and colleges to team up. To understand this phenomenon, we must look to the origins and nature of the historical relationships between secondary and postsecondary institutions in our nation's very loosely linked educational system.

THE HISTORY OF HIGH SCHOOL AND
COLLEGE RELATIONSHIPS: A Legacy of Distrust

Partnerships in Practice

The literature on high school-college partnerships is replete
with less than optimistic but colorful descriptions of obstacles
to attempts at articulation between high schools and colleges.
The American educational edifice has been described as being
built upon a kind of San Andreas Fault, with schools and colleges residing on either side of the fault line (Frost 1972).
Snyder (1974, p.1) refers to a Maginot line, Stanfield (1981,
p. 45) in a mixed metaphor, describes a "gulf . . . oceans wide
and decades long," Greenberg (1982, p. 79) speaks of an
abyss, while Boyer describes "a game of tug of war in which
schools and colleges are adversaries" (1983, p. 225).

The discovery that collaboration does not occur naturally
across institutional lines neither is recent nor trivial. As this
chapter will demonstrate, recognizing partnerships as unnat-
urally occurring phenomena has provided the impetus for
most of the significant events that have occurred in the arena
of school-college partnerships since 1855.

School-College Articulation: A Historical Perspective

After the American Revolution, this nation's educational institutions at the secondary and postsecondary levels developed
nearly totally independently of one another. Early educators
eschewed centralized control, yet heavily were influenced
by European traditions still highly esteemed in the newly
formed United States. Little overriding control was exerted
by the states—still less from the federal government. Educating beyond the level of basic literacy was the nearly exclusive province of the social elite and the privileged (Bender
1986). As a loosely coupled enterprise—one that resists a
national consensus on process and outcomes—education still
is very much a current concern despite the intervening centuries of heated debate (Chira 1991).

Nearly 80 years later in 1855, the New England Association
of College and Preparatory Schools was formed to improve
communication, admissions procedures, curriculum coordination, and high school certification among member
schools (Menacker 1975). This was the first of many events
which initiated what the Carnegie Commission called "the
search for a coordinated system" (1973, p. 1).

Individual states also were beginning to see the wisdom
in asserting some order on arrangements between schools

and colleges. Stoel cites as two early examples Michigan for its 1870 effort to set admissions standards for high school graduates seeking admission to the University of Michigan and New York for its attempt to standardize the college-preparation curriculum by creating in 1878 a comprehensive system of statewide Regents Examinations (pp. 15–16).

In 1892, the Committee of Ten (Rippa 1976, p. 307) issued its widely distributed report recommending that secondary schools strictly adhere to a uniform college-preparatory curriculum (Menacker 1975, p. 15). The report also recommended the Carnegie Unit be adopted, even though the Carnegie Foundation's committee stated quite specifically that "in counting [units of credits], the fundamental criterion was the amount of time spent on the subject, not the results attained" (Gerhard 1955, p. 658).

In another attempt to standardize the college admissions process, in 1910 the Middle States Association was formed in part to develop external exams for member colleges to use; this led to the creation of the College Entrance Examination Board.

Partially in response to these associations, the Committee of Nine was formed in 1910. The committee advocated less rigidity in the college-preparatory high school curriculum and the development of a more general concurrent program in high schools applicable to an increasingly diverse student population.

In 1926, the College Entrance Examination Board introduced the Scholastic Aptitude Test and suggested that colleges use it in place of the external examinations they traditionally had used to determine student preparedness for admission. The use for the first time of a normed test of "general aptitude" was a historic event and seemed a way to satisfy the colleges' need to assess students who came increasingly from diverse high school curriculum experiences. Because the test was general in nature—especially when compared with the highly idiosyncratic external examinations—high school educators believed they could offer students a flexible curriculum and still prepare them adequately for the SAT. The SAT gained steadily in national acceptance, and by the 1940s it generally was used (Menacker 1975, p. 18).

While secondary school educators believed a more flexible route to a high school diploma was the correct one, empirical evidence to support this belief was not yet available. In 1930, the Progressive Education Association appointed the Commission on the Relation of School to College; this commission conducted what came to be known as the Eight-Year Study. Surprisingly, the commission found that high school students who had learned under a nontraditional curriculum were superior to their college-preparatory counterparts in nearly all matters under study, including scholastic average, grades, honors achieved, motivation, curiosity, rates of graduation from college, and postcollege plans (Rippa 1976, p. 323).

The impact of the findings of the Eight-Year Study—especially on the postsecondary world—was profound. According to Menacker, "It demonstrated that secondary schools were competent to develop their own curricula for a diverse high school population that included the college bound. Colleges did not have to direct the high schools as if secondary educators were less intelligent components of the educational system. . . . Teachers at both levels came to realize that neither approach to admissions fully resolved transitional problems and that the best solutions would be realized only through cooperative efforts" (1975, p. 17).

The use for the first time of a normed test of "general aptitude" was a historic event. . . .

Early departures from "12 + 4"

Nearly all of the history recounted thus far has dealt with the way high schools and colleges worked at fashioning a lexicon and syntax for articulation. The need for clear communication became evident to both sets of institutions as they observed the increasing number and growing diversity of students moving on to college from high school.

Prior to the early 1950s, however, only a few historically noteworthy efforts had been mounted to examine the basic structure and assumptions of the "12 + 4" arrangement of precollegiate and postsecondary study. These efforts, the Three Year Program at Harvard (Van Gelder 1972); Johns Hopkins' Three Year Collegiate Program (Spurr 1970; Bersi 1973); and efforts at the University of Chicago (Spurr 1970; Stoel 1988), involved the concept of acceleration, defined by Pressey in 1949 as "progress through an educational program faster or at ages younger than convention."

These programs as well as later experiments in the 1950s involved an exclusive subset of the student population: the academically gifted.

Models of student acceleration in the 1950s

The onset of the Korean conflict in the early 1950s and the deepening Cold War between the United States and the Soviet Union heightened the urgency to increase military and technological development and led to a call for the universal conscription of all 18-year-olds. In response, colleges pressured high schools to accelerate high-performing students into college at earlier ages (Maeroff 1983, p. 15).

Five models for student acceleration were underwritten by the Ford Foundation through its Fund for the Advancement of Education. Each model is described in the fund's report, "Bridging the Gap Between School and College" (1953). Three projects are particularly noteworthy. The Program for Early Admission to College demonstrated that gifted 16-year-old high school students could enroll full time at rigorous colleges and succeed academically (the Fund for the Advancement of Education 1957; Miller 1968). The Harvard/Exeter Program and the Kenyon Plan (Townsend 1980) led directly to the creation of the Advanced Placement Program.

In 1955, the Advanced Placement Program came under the formal aegis of the College Entrance Examination Board. Today it stands as the single largest program of its kind in the nation (Hanson 1980, pp. 10-11).

A truce in the articulation wars: Something for everyone

As the articulation issue moved into the 1960s, a period of relative quiescence occurred. The status quo as perceived by both secondary and postsecondary players in the articulation game seemed to give relative comfort to all concerned. Secondary school leaders faced an era of social turmoil and calls for greater curriculum relevance. However, they found themselves operating in an environment in which almost any possible innovation was greeted at least with acceptance by parents and taxpayers who were frightened by the social pressures unleashed by the nation's schoolgoing youth.

Additionally, secondary school communications with colleges and universities—on the surface, at least—seemed to be as good as necessary. Much had been addressed over the preceding century or so: Carnegie Units, the SATs, the ACTs, and the College Entrance Examination Board's Achievement Tests were evidence. Agreements between the National Association of Secondary School Principals and college admissions organizations that covered using class rank, high school averages, and standardized achievement test scores as determinants in the college admissions process served as testament as well.

Despite the proceedings of the Committee of Ten, high schools still had great flexibility in educating the college bound. The AP program provided the capstone to articulation efforts, as it permitted high schools to offer at little or no expense college-level preparation to the most able portion of the student body while at the same time upgrading the general community's perception of the secondary school program.

Colleges, too, might have been justified in feeling some degree of satisfaction with the state of articulation affairs. The standardization assumed by the nationwide adoption of the Carnegie Unit along with the general use of standardized admissions testing permitted the colleges to make admissions decisions about applicants who represented a diverse roster of academic preparation, range in skills, and breadth of socioeconomic status that simply was unmatched in any previous era.

Articulation, however, entered a new—and again contentious—stage. A number of factors combined in the 1970s and 1980s to move the issue of high school-college partnerships off the back burner of complacency into a crucible of public and professional scrutiny and reassessment. Such factors included issues vigorously raised initially in the Carnegie Commission's report, "Continuity and Discontinuity: Higher Education and the Schools" (1973), and developed in later reformist policy papers; popular concerns over the relative worth and competitiveness of American education when compared to other industrialized nations; the continuing failure of schools and colleges to adequately address issues of access and equity; and continuing social unrest.

Secondary and postsecondary policy makers needed to consider a major issue. In light of the tortuous path leading to even the most basic understandings and working agreements developed by the late 1960s, was ambitious, meaningful, collaborative high school-college continuum restructuring even possible? After all, it already had been a very long, bumpy trip.

COOPERATIVE OR COLLABORATIVE PARTNERSHIPS: More Than a Semantic Difference

If today's buzz word is collaboration, we clearly must under-stand what the word does and does not represent within the context of high school-college relations. Not all joint activities between colleges and secondary schools truly are collabor-ative, nor perhaps should they be. Before discussing, it must be understood that collaboration is merely a subset—albeit an important one—of articulation.

Defining Articulation

Although it might be taken for granted that high school-college partnership efforts conveniently and appropriately can be grouped under the heading of "articulation activities," practitioners might not be surprised to learn that articulation has been defined and redefined many times over the years. One writer refers to articulation as "the method or process of joining together. It is a procedure that should provide a continuous, smooth flow of students from school to school. The need to develop a systematic procedure for student prog-ress, with particular reference to integration of instructional programs, is implicit in the transfer process. In its broadest meaning, articulation refers to interrelationships among the various levels and segments of an educational system as well as among off-campus quasi-educational in situations and activ-ities. Segments of an educational system may be considered well articulated if these interrelationships operate as a unified process" (Kintzer 1973, p. 1).

Blanchard broadens and enhances the Kintzer definition: He states that articulated programs enhance opportunities for students to fulfill their intellectual potential while address-ing their emotional, social, physical, mental, and spiritual needs (1975).

When the lenses of various definitions converge, a common focus emerges: a concern for smooth, unimpeded progress between successive institutional levels. In this way, students can make the most of their individual growth potential while meeting needs in cognitive, physiological, emotional, social, and other areas.

Yet, even as this emerging consensus is being reported, it is perhaps as interesting to examine what is not directly stated or implied in any of the foregoing definitions. All of the pre-vious definitions in one way or another suggest linkages between schools and colleges—that is, sending and receiving institutions. It is students that are sent and received, and we hope they are armed with the sort of preparation that both types of institutions have agreed will stand the students in good stead.

This presupposes, however, that articulation concerns itself chiefly with moving and preparing high school students for collegiate programs and the attendant issues. As it turns out, significant and growing areas of joint activity are organized between schools and colleges. These activities are concerned with other populations and objectives and will be described in later sections which focus on program models.

Contemporary articulation efforts, it can be argued, can and should—indeed, already do—extend beyond the traditional areas defined for such undertakings. Out of the swelling of publications, conferences, programs, and policy on local, state, and national levels—initiated by schools and colleges, professional organizations, state legislatures, and departments of education—a broadened appreciation has emerged of all partnership activities as legitimate parts of articulation efforts. Has the nature of the process of these partnerships altered significantly from earlier efforts? Are these efforts collaborative, as often claimed? Perhaps the place to start is with an explanation of what is meant by collaboration.

Cooperation and Collaboration

While some researchers believe the words "collaboration" and "cooperation" fundamentally are interchangeable (Intriligator 1983, p. 5), others believe the level of involvement in collaborating agencies or institutions is more intense than in cooperative relationships. For example, Kenneth Hoyt, the former director of the Office of Career Education, defines cooperation as "a term that assumes two or more parties, each with separate and autonomous programs, agree to work together in making all programs more successful" (1978, p. 8).

He defines collaboration, on the other hand, as "a term that implies the parties involved share responsibility and authority for basic policy decision making" (1978, p. 9).

One of the more satisfying definitions of collaboration has been developed by Shaffer and Bryant, who define it as "shared decision making in governance, planning, delivery, and evaluation of programs. It is a pluralistic form of education where people of dissimilar back grounds work together with equal status. It may be seen as working with rather than working on a person" (1983, p. 3).

Applying the definitions of cooperation and collaboration offered here, many of the articulated efforts described in later chapters will be characterized as cooperative rather than collaborative. That is, most involve separate entities working together but typically not relinquishing individual decision-making power and authority.

This is not surprising, since as Shaffer and Bryant contend, "collaboration is necessary and valuable, but . . . it occurs only in special settings or in unusual circumstances" (1983, p. 6). Going still further, Beckhard maintains that in order for collaboration to occur, "there must be real dissatisfaction with the status quo, a high enough level of dissatisfaction to mobilize energy toward some change" (1975, p. 424).

Despite the various points of view incorporated into these definitions and theories, agreement appears evident that in order for collaborations to succeed, support must be directed from the highest institutional levels (Ascher 1988, p. 23; Mocker, Martin, and Brown 1986).

One can argue that not all partnerships need to be collaborations; cooperation, as defined above, may also be viewed as a positive and in many cases the most appropriate partnership form. In other cases, partners who have reached Beckhard's "point of dissatisfaction" actually might wish to collaborate and yet find obstacles, typically unanticipated, which prevent them from realizing their goals.

The power of these hidden impediments needs to be understood and appreciated fully by both high school and college faculty, staff, and administrative leaders if collaborations are to be formed in more than name only. The road to failed partnerships too often has been paved merely with good intentions. Would-be collaborators and cooperators would be wise not to underestimate the potential—but not insurmountable—disruptive power of the discontinuity between high school and college cultures.

HIGH SCHOOL AND COLLEGE CULTURAL DISCONTINUITY:
Latent Antagonist to Successful Partnerships

Despite the obvious interest and discussion surrounding efforts at high school-college collaboration, the number of successful efforts seems to represent a relatively small portion of high schools and colleges. Those that have succeeded, such as the effort to replicate LaGuardia Community College's frequently cited concurrent-enrollment model, Middle College High School, have required extensive technical assistance, time, patience, and often heroic support from decision makers at all institutional levels (Cullen and Moed 1988; Quality Education 1990, p. 69).

If partnership efforts both are desirable and beneficial, why has progress been slower and more difficult than many policy makers and practitioners anticipated? Perhaps some portion of this phenomenon might be explained by examining the cultural forces at play in both the high school and postsecondary venues.

While some prominent observers have commented on the general cultural discontinuity between colleges and high schools, few have cataloged and explained those cultural manifestations which most often arise to impede crosscultural collaboration. The significance of exploring in detail this area derives from the belief that being aware of these cultural differences prior to the collaborative effort will help participants to understand some of the customs, applications, procedures, and beliefs held dear in the academic cultures of their counterparts. This knowledge can be crucial to attributing informed meaning to the language and behavior of negotiating partners. In its absence, would-be partners might be all too likely to attribute obstructionist motives to otherwise benign behavior.

For the sake of analysis, it is possible to group these "cultural indicators" into several categories: institutional funding and resources; the student body; teachers and teaching conditions; valuing performance; faculty role in decision making; and institutional leadership style.

Institutional Funding and Resources

While generalizations always are subject to local exception, high schools usually are supported by tax-levy funds raised through real estate taxes (Garms, Guthrie, and Pierce 1978, p. 132). These funds most often specifically must be approved by school district residents, and allocated based in part on upon average daily student attendance or average daily student register. Public colleges usually are supported by operating or general funds of the municipality, county, or state, not typically tied to ballot-box approval. Operating funds, at least in large part, very often are allocated based upon the number of equated full-time equivalent (FTE) students registered on a designated census date—not based upon daily attendance (Cohen and Brawer 1989, pp. 130-133).

Both public and private colleges usually derive part of their operating support from student tuition and fees. The burden to students often is offset partially or completely by financial aid programs. Public high schools generally may not levy tuition or fees.

College students are expected to pay for books, consumable materials, and sometimes specialized, course-specific equipment. High schools are expected to provide these "essentials" to students at public expense.

Secondary and postsecondary institutions both seek and receive state, federal, and foundation grant support. Secondary schools tend to win a greater proportion of such funding from entitlement programs with relatively few major awards from competitive grant programs. Colleges typically are involved heavily in competitive grant competitions and receive a higher percentage of their grant funds from these nonentitlement sources as compared to secondary school systems.

Finally, colleges—and especially private colleges—seek and receive endowments from a variety of private sources: individual donors, foundations, and corporations. These funds are used to supplement other sources of income for either restricted or nonrestricted use.

For all these reasons, college administrators typically enjoy a much greater degree of fiscal flexibility and autonomy than do their secondary school counterparts. College administrators frequently are surprised and annoyed at the apparent lack of fiscal ingenuity shown by high school partners. It is important for colleges to understand that often the requirement for more stringent public accountability, rather than a lack of creativity, leads to this perception.

The Student Body

Many differences exist within the characteristics of high school and college student bodies. Some are self-evident, while others are less obvious. In all cases, however, the nature of the student body has a great deal to do with the nature of the respective high school and college cultures.

Differences can be found in the respective students' age ranges, ethnicity, gender, and degree of choice over schools to attend, curriculum, and living arrangements. Because college students usually are older, better prepared academically, more mature and independent, and able to exercise greater choice over their curriculum than high school students, it follows that colleges as institutions tend to be more open and flexible than high schools in most aspects of operation, including articulation.

Teachers and Teaching

Much of what is different about high schools and colleges derives from the respective student bodies. Teaching also profoundly affects and in many ways defines the cultural boundaries between the secondary and postsecondary worlds. In many respects, teaching conditions, expectations, ambience, and to some degree even career satisfaction are arguably produced by the interaction of student characteristics and the organizational scope and structure of secondary schools and higher education.

Because teaching is, after all, the major service-delivery area of schools and colleges and because this area is the preoccupation and responsibility of the single largest class of professional employees in both sets of institutions, it is especially important for those who might wish to form partnerships to be informed about the differences in the lives of high school and college teachers. Generally, college faculty have lighter teaching loads, meaning fewer classes, contact hours and students. Class size, with the exception of lectures, also tends to be smaller. However, recent trends in higher education funding, especially at public institutions, have increased class sizes. College students, again generally, are prepared better academically, have chosen specific institutions and classes, and require less faculty intervention regarding their classroom deportment.

College faculty also typically enjoy greater latitude than do high school teachers in selecting instructional materials such as textbooks and other supplies. Individual faculty members often are permitted to decide which texts to use. Additionally, because students purchase books with their own funds, few opportunities exist for outside authorities under state or local auspices to interfere in selecting texts or to take issue with

Generally, college faculty have lighter teaching loads, meaning fewer classes, contact hours and students.

contents of the texts themselves.

High school teachers, while sometimes consulted in selecting texts, are more likely to find themselves using books that have been purchased with scarce public money (often resulting in outdated texts, especially in the science and social sciences areas), selected by school administrators—often from limited preapproved state lists.

Another distinguishing feature is academic freedom. The tradition of academic freedom much more firmly is ingrained in the academy than it is in secondary schools (Reutter 1985, p. 152). Secondary school teachers, although they may exercise some degree of control over professional choices, do not prevail when their own judgments conflict with the policies of their principal or school board. This contrasts sharply with the belief in and exercise of academic freedom in colleges. For example, a significant portion of a defense of tenure for college professors can be framed in academic freedom issues. Says Rosovsky, "Tenure is the principal guarantor of academic freedom, ensuring the right to teach what one believes, to espouse unpopular academic and nonacademic causes, to act upon knowledge and ideas as one perceives them without fear of retribution from anyone" (1990, pp. 179-80).

Whether one teaches in high school or college also has a significant impact on salary and vacation time. College teachers tend to earn more and enjoy greater segments of time away from teaching (Average Faculty Salaries 1990). All told, the college teacher's work year is approximately 30 weeks long, while the secondary school teacher's is usually 40 weeks long.

Like so many other factors, the amenities surrounding the teaching staff at high schools and colleges tend to differ substantially. College faculty enjoy greater office space, access to phones, clerical support, and freedom of movement. All of these elements can lend obstacles, both interpersonal and professional, to high school and college faculty who are asked to collaborate on a project. For example, it is very hard for a college professor with easy access to a phone or a good message system to comprehend the difficulties most high school teachers experience when they receive a phone call at school.

With respect to teaching qualifications, both secondary and college teachers are subject-area specialists, and both groups have undergraduate majors in areas related to the areas in which they teach. However, with the rare exception of a few community colleges in which teachers might not hold professorial rank, college teachers are not required by either state departments of education or their employing colleges to have completed pedagogical courses. Teachers who work in colleges and universities are not required to be licensed or certified by states, accrediting agencies, or local entities, while secondary school teachers, again almost without exception, are required to be licensed or certified by a state education department or a local board of education. Differences in preparation and the lack of secondary school flexibility in certification can lead to real difficulties in hiring key nontraditional personnel to work in secondary schools as part of a partnership effort.

In almost every aspect, the act of and environment surrounding college teaching contrasts sharply with the experience of the typical high school teacher. These differences, unfortunately, often can be the wellspring of feelings of envy, jealousy, insecurity, superiority, mistrust, and misunderstanding when faculty from high schools and colleges are asked to collaborate.

Valuing Performance

In some cases, high schools and colleges claim to value areas in common; in others, no overlap exists. Even those areas which might be valued in both cultures, however, sometimes are defined differently and divergently evaluated. Both colleges and high schools publicly value the quality of instruction but use different techniques to evaluate it. In colleges, peer observation and student evaluations widely are used, while in high schools, the predominant methodology remains supervisor observation. In addition, when making promotion and tenure decisions, colleges place much greater value than do high schools on research, publishing, collegiality, grants development, and service on faculty committees.

Faculty Role in Decision Making

The roles of high school teachers and college faculty vary markedly with regard to types of decisions they might make and their degree of involvement. College faculty often play a greater role in institutional governance, controlling course content, selecting textbooks, selecting departmental chairs, developing and enforcing student disciplinary codes, and supervising and evaluating peers than do their high school colleagues.

Institutional Leadership Style

The manner in which leadership is exercised tends to vary greatly by level. This section illustrates some of these disparities which necessarily are as much reflections of unique institutional cultures as they are contributors to those cultures.

Principal/president

High school principals and college presidents come to their positions via different routes. College presidents often are selected after successful careers as scholars and researchers followed by terms as academic officers. Another route to the college presidency is via a distinguished public career. Two examples here are John Brademas, who became president of New York University after a successful career in Congress, and Thomas Keane, who assumed the presidency of Drew University after two popular terms as governor of New Jersey.

High school principals typically have less spectacular backgrounds. While nearly all have begun their careers in the classroom, many have distinguished themselves less as academic leaders than in administrative or athletic leadership roles. Many high school principals have been coaches and athletic directors or deans of discipline prior to assuming their positions.

Because principals and presidents come to their positions from such different paths, it is not surprising that they should take different approaches to the exercise of institutional leadership.

Leadership process

Principals tend to be involved intimately in the short-term planning and day-to-day administration of their high schools. Much of their day is spent reacting to the events surrounding them. Little time is spent on long-term planning—a point not intended as a criticism. The institution looks to the principal to resolve disputes between staff members, teachers, and students. A great deal of paper must be moved and the principal is expected to exercise control over a myriad of other day-to-day administrative activities.

Additionally, principals also must observe and evaluate their teaching staff and assistant principals; they are responsible for implementing mandated curricula; and they usually are held accountable directly for the academic achievement of students by the public, the superintendent, and the school board.

College presidents tend to be more involved in long-range planning, fundamental allocation of strategic resources, external relationships, development, and executive-level staffing. In short, they more frequently are concerned with policies and the broader institutional ramifications of implementation than they are with the details and practices of implementation itself. The academic areas of the college must, by the nature of the traditions of academic freedom, be managed less directly and more consensually than in high schools.

All of these characteristics tend to lead toward a more reflective, process-oriented leadership style in colleges and a more reactive, take-charge attitude on the part of principals. Most successful college presidents learn to respect the power of the process; most college faculty will be offended deeply if they regularly are excluded from the process.

Change in college tends to result from a great deal of consultation and frequently much negotiating as well. When dealing with college counterparts, high school personnel often are confused about who is in charge—after all, in high schools someone always is in charge. To them, it seems as if everyone—and at the same time no one—is the leader on the college campus.

Board of trustees/school board

The powers delegated to principals and presidents by school boards and trustees, respectively, actually are reflected in the general approach the institutional leaders take in carrying out their tasks. Trustees usually advise presidents; they rarely order them. Presidents are, in turn, expected to provide board members with an accurate sense of the institution and lay out directions for future growth and development. Once these directions are accepted by the trustees, they will in ordinary circumstances allow the president wide latitude and ample time to follow them. Of course, institutions in crisis tend to precipitate more active trustee involvement.

School boards often have difficulty limiting their involvement with policy and practice. They generally are more involved than college trustees in monitoring the implementation of policy, and they demand both a closer working relationship with the principal and more frequent updates about school initiatives.

The contrasting autonomy (or lack thereof) of high school and college leaders has an obvious impact on the nature of the collaborative process which, depending on one's institutional perspective, might seem hopelessly complicated and attenuated.

Considering all these factors, however, it must be emphasized that discontinuities notwithstanding, principals and presidents must play absolutely essential roles if crossinstitutional collaboratives are ever to take hold. The degree to which these pivotal players regard and embrace each other signals to other institutional players the extent to which they are expected to value, respect, and collaborate with their opposite numbers (Parnell 1985, p. 119). Inevitably, without such exercises of leadership, petty jealousies, mistrust, turf battles, and feelings of inferiority or superiority could arise to taint and ultimately doom the process.

CONCURRENT-ENROLLMENT MODELS

What is Concurrent Enrollment?

Concurrent enrollment occurs when students are permitted to enroll in college-level courses prior to their graduation from high school. Students often receive credit toward their high school diploma while simultaneously receiving college credit for their successful efforts in these college-level courses. Concurrent-enrollment programs also are called joint- or dual-enrollment programs.

Why Is Concurrent Enrollment Important Today?

It probably is not coincidental that high school-college articulation is an important consideration in an era of renewed scrutiny of national education provided. The climate of educational inquiry and reform has been fueled by a number of factors that have combined to create an active audience for the debate on how well our "system" of secondary and postsecondary education works. These factors include increasing college tuition costs, public skepticism about the value of increased secondary school spending, debate over the purpose of college and the meaning of cultural literacy, and a teacher shortage. A series of reports included *A Nation at Risk* (National Commission on Excellence in Education 1983), which heightened the public perception of a crisis in our schools.

Throughout this debate, thoughtful critics such as Theodore Sizer (1984) and Dale Parnell (1985), among many others, as well as major secondary and postsecondary organizations have called for the ways students move between high schools and colleges to be reexamined and identified the bridges that need to be built between both sets of institutions.

As discussed in Section 1, these individuals and groups as well as others have focused on two major areas of articulation concern: secondary-postsecondary curricular redundancy and changes in the nature of the college population.

Affording Greater College Access

Along with continuing curricular redundancy and a more mature student body, another development has enhanced the significance of concurrent-enrollment programs. Over the course of many years and for a variety of reasons, colleges began to open their doors to a much broader array of students. Most colleges no longer are the exclusive preserves of the intellectual and social elite. As a result of the demo-

cratization of college admissions, today's first-year college student class more closely reflects the broad range of ability and achievement of the nation's high school graduates.

This is confirmed by examining the data. For example, 2,650,000 students graduated in June 1985 from high schools in the United States (Rothman 1986). In September 1985, approximately 50 percent of those students entered this country's 2,100 two- and four-year colleges (Boyer 1987, p. 1). Even if all the students in the top decile of the graduating class attended college after graduating high school, more than one million low to moderate achievers also attended. Yet, historically, the entering class as a whole has maintained a mean grade of C+ during the freshman year (Ramist 1984, p. 163).

Clearly, then, many students who graduate high school each June go on to college a scant three months later and succeed, even though they have not necessarily been in the highest achieving group in secondary school. This has had a significant impact on the recent development of concurrent-enrollment programs, especially with respect to potential target populations. Prior to this understanding, college-level study in high school had been the narrow province of the most intellectually talented, highest achieving students, a practice with historically intuitive appeal. Students of low to moderate levels of achievement had never been given the opportunity to participate in dual-enrollment programs. Why, specifically, had these students been excluded? Do the reasons bear up under closer scrutiny?

Reasons Cited for Excluding Moderate Achievers From College Study in High School

The traditional justification to exclude moderate-achieving students from college-level study in high school is that these students are not bright, skilled, and motivated enough to cope with the demands of college course work. Their collegiate success after high school graduation, however, seems to deny the validity of this argument. Furthermore, other researchers who specifically have studied the performance of moderate achievers in joint-enrollment programs have found that students in these programs generally do quite well in their college courses (Greenberg 1987; Suss and Goldsmith 1989).

Other reasons for exclusion, perhaps less pointed, have been offered from a variety of sources. For example, some critics fear the negative motivational consequence of "rewarding" moderate-achieving high school students with the privilege of taking college courses. Others worry that providing college study for some moderate achievers will lead to demands for the same opportunity for all, prompting the attendant runaway costs. Some are concerned that expanding opportunities will increase administrative entanglements and "red tape" between high schools and colleges. Finally, some economists cite trends that point to increased employment possibilities for janitors, secretaries, store clerks, and other low-status positions. They believe that encouraging "average" students to go on to college is not in the nation's best economic interest. These "average" students otherwise would be the backbone of the work force needed to fill the slots in these unattractive yet economically important areas of the production function.

Despite all these arguments, the apparent inequity of exclusion has led educators to design joint-enrollment programs that can serve students of moderate or even below-average achievement while continuing to serve the needs of the gifted. As a result, the pool of students eligible to participate in and benefit from these programs today has increased dramatically. It is, therefore, more important than ever that educators and policy makers understand the implications and potential benefits of concurrent-enrollment programs.

Benefits of Concurrent-Enrollment Programs

The potential benefits of concurrent-enrollment programs—and the costs of denying moderately achieving students access to such programs—are numerous and substantial. Students, parents, high schools, colleges, and society as a whole might prosper from broader application of dual-enrollment designs.

The benefits to students are considerable. The most obvious is that students who participate in concurrent-enrollment programs have the chance to earn college credit while still in high school. This permits students, once in college, to accelerate through the college program more quickly (also possibly reducing tuition costs) or to opt for additional electives or courses in highly specialized areas earlier in their college careers.

Properly designed to meet the needs of students of either moderate or above-average ability, concurrent-enrollment programs can provide great inspiration as well as affirmation of their ability to succeed at the college level. Finally, concurrent enrollment also can provide a cure for senior boredom.

Parents can benefit by concurrent-enrollment models in two principal ways. First, they might save money, since students can pass one or more college-level courses during their senior year of high school, which means a potential tuition savings when the student enters college. Second, parents who might doubt the ability or motivation of their child to successfully cope with college-level study will have a chance to learn how prepared their children really are.

Setting up joint enrollment programs can result in many pluses for high schools. First, offering seniors an intellectually challenging college-level experience—with its concomitant financial advantages—can be a powerful alternative for school administrators in combating "senioritis." Second, by making joint enrollment possible for more students and more diverse student types, a high school can bring off a real community relations coup.

Third, in the process of creating dual-enrollment programs, high schools and colleges necessarily have to open lines of communication which might not have existed previously. This can result in closer relations among high school college advisors and cooperating colleges, college scholars available to guest lecture, and joint curriculum projects.

The High school faculty

Fourth, the impact on high school teachers can be especially positive and profound. Depending on the selected concurrent-enrollment model, high school teaching faculty might become involved as college adjunct faculty either on the high school campus or at the college. The spinoffs of this are manifold and include extra compensation from the college for special teaching duties, interaction at the highest professional levels with colleagues from their own academic disciplines, opportunities to participate in professional development, and positive effects on teacher morale and self-concept.

Colleges typically offer several reasons for getting involved in dual-enrollment programs. Student recruitment is most frequently cited. In a partnership with a local high school, a college has access to students, their families, and, perhaps as importantly, their counselors, college advisors, and teachers. In addition, links between high schools and colleges present unique grant-writing possibilities for colleges, especially in the areas of teacher training and development, increasing the pool of minority teaching applicants, curriculum development, technical and vocational training, replication of concurrent-enrollment models, and enrollment of first-generation college students.

Another mutually satisfying outcome is that high school teachers can be brought up to date by college faculty on research issues in their respective fields. In turn, high school teachers offer insights to the college faculty into current high school curriculum practices and the level of preparation of high school seniors. Joint curriculum planning, often otherwise next to impossible due to jurisdictional disputes, now can occur to the benefit of all, supported by a collegiality otherwise unlikely.

Finally, concurrent-enrollment programs are a community relations bonanza for a college: The college is seen playing a constructive role in helping students through the local high school.

Joint-enrollment programs also can contribute to the society at large. Students with the greatest ability can begin advanced study earlier in their college careers if they've earned credit in freshman courses before graduation from high school. But the untapped power and benefit to society might be in the special role these programs can play for the more average student as well as for minority and economically disadvantaged students. Consider the loss to our nation in terms of human potential if capable students allow their futures to be guided by unrealistically low expectations and never enter college.

Because academic performance and curriculum tracking are so closely associated with race and income, the challenge to completing what Ernest Boyer calls "the unfinished agenda of access and equity" is great. He says: "To expand access without upgrading schools is simply to perpetuate discrimination in a more subtle form. But to push for excellence in ways that ignore the needs of less privileged students is to undermine the future of the nation. Clearly, equity and excellence cannot be divided" (Boyer 1983, p. 6).

Nearly 30 years ago, the director of the College Scholarship Service, Rexford G. Moon, estimated that the nation was "losing the talents of 150,000 able youths a year from the lower income levels . . . who for one reason or another do not continue their education beyond high school" (Sexton 1961, p. 187). Today, this still is a grave concern. For example, between 1980 and 1985, black enrollment in colleges

The college is seen playing a constructive role in helping students through the local high school.

declined at a time when enrollment for all other groups rose (Rothman 1986). Boyer again put it succinctly: "Opportunity remains unequal. And this failure to educate every young person to his or her full potential threatens the nation's social and economic health" (1987, p. 5). It is in this context that the significance of joint-enrollment programs for moderate-achieving students emerges. Such programs represent not merely an early opportunity to earn college credit, but symbolize society's commitment to equity and access—not only for the most advantaged or gifted—but for everyone.

Conceptual Models for Concurrent-Enrollment Programs

While many variations on the concurrent-enrollment theme are possible, the following table covers the major conceptual models.

Models of Concurrent-Enrollment Design

CURRICULAR DESIGN

WHO TEACHES	Special Course		Regular Course	
College Faculty	1h	1c	2h	2c
High School Faculty	3h	3c	4h	4c

h: Course taught on high school campus
c: Course taught on college campus

In this matrix, models 1 and 2 involve college faculty teaching courses that are either regular college courses (model 2) or specially designed college courses (model 1), while models 3 and 4 represent, respectively, adapted college courses or regular college courses taught by high school faculty. Courses, whether taught by high school or college faculty, may be taught, depending on locally agreed-upon arrangements, on the college campus (c) or at the high school (h).

It also is possible in any one concurrent-enrollment program for aspects of two or more designs to be incorporated.

The significance of these distinctions and the conceptual models for dual-enrollment programs will be amplified in the individual program descriptions which follow.

Examples of Concurrent-Enrollment Programs

This segment offers descriptions and analyses of several approaches to concurrent enrollment. Some are initiated locally and only involve a single high school and a single college. Others exist on either a state, regional, or national level. The programs represent a cross section of intended populations (students at risk to high achievers), institutional types (private and public high schools and colleges), initiating points (state legislatures, private agencies, and local schools and colleges), and geographic areas.

Perhaps one reason for the variety of concurrent-enrollment programs is the ebb and flow between colleges, high schools, national programs, local boards of education, state departments of education, and local and state legislative bodies over the efficacy of and funding for these models. The familiar aphorism of "the money follows the kids" sometimes has been changed to "the money follows the kind of credit (college or high school) granted." This clearly is demonstrated in the evolution of the Minnesota Postsecondary Options program, described herein.

It should be noted that while each of these programs might be viewed as an archetype, many variations of the programs presented here not only are possible, but already exist; also, not all archetypes are represented here due to space limitations.

College-level course experiences
For high school students

The Advanced Placement program. No discussion of contemporary high school-college cooperation or collaboration can be considered complete without discussing the College Entrance Examination Board's Advanced Placement (AP) program.

The AP is long established and well researched. It is, arguably, the best known and most broadly implemented program of its model type (3h).

AP became a formal program of the College Board* in 1955 after an experimental period under the auspices of several private colleges and universities. At its inception, AP was

*College Board, 45 Columbus Ave., New York, NY 10023-6917; (212) 713-8000.

intended to bring college faculty and high school teachers together, to motivate and reward able and ambitious students, to concentrate on curricular design and course content, and to offer the alternative to well-prepared students of college-level study. Although the program served only 1,229 students in 104 schools in its first year (Hanson 1980, p. 9), AP has grown substantially since that time. Today it serves more than 200,000 students in about one-third of the nation's schools.

The AP program permits high schools across the country to offer classes in which the curricula has been designed concurrently by high school and college educators to provide college-level study geared to standardized tests. The tests are prepared by groups of high school and college educators under the supervision of the Educational Testing Service. The courses are taught in high schools by local high school faculty who usually have received training at College Board-sponsored workshops.

Students earn high school credit for successfully completing an AP course but do not automatically receive college credit for that course. Rather, those who desire college credit must take the AP exam and then submit their test results to the colleges they might wish to attend following high school graduation.

The AP examinations are graded on a scale of one to five: Five equals "extremely well qualified for college credit"; four equals "well qualified"; three equals "qualified"; two equals "possibly qualified"; one equals "no recommendation." Colleges may at their option either accept or reject AP exam scores and are not compelled to grant credit for even the highest scores achieved. Some colleges will grant college credit earned through AP in lieu of their own freshman courses. Other colleges might grant elective credit but still mandate students to take the college's required courses in those same areas. Some colleges will not grant college credit based on AP work but will grant advance standing in a subject area. A few colleges will grant neither college credit nor advanced standing.

The students attracted to the AP program clearly are above average even when compared to their peers—high school seniors who intend to apply to college. Evidence for this conclusion abounds. For example, although the mean verbal and math Scholastic Aptitude Test scores in 1979 for all graduating seniors were 421 and 462, respectively, AP students had mean scores of 555 and 594 (Hanson 1980).

Additionally, achievement test scores were higher for AP students than for other students taking the achievement tests, and AP students showed much greater interest in attaining graduate degrees than the college-bound senior group taken as a whole.

The AP program has many virtues. Chief among these are the following:

1. The program is widely known, recognized, mature, and generally accepted.
2. Students earning scores of three or better have a very good likelihood of earning college credit for their efforts in colleges and universities throughout the nation.
3. Students who take AP courses frequently are regarded by college admissions personnel as more attractive than their peers, who otherwise might be equally qualified, but who have not taken part in the program.
4. The program can be implemented at little cost, in most cases without restructuring the school day for students or faculty. Although the College Board recommends a class maximum of 25, adherence to this guideline is at the option of local school authorities.
5. Even students who might not score high enough on the AP exam to earn college credit (or who might not choose to sit for the exam at all) benefit by experiencing rigorous, college-level work, which is good preparation for the collegiate experience.
6. Teachers who administer the AP course become part of a network of colleagues—locally, regionally, and nationally—who attend workshops, read and contribute to newsletters, revise curricula, design and grade AP exams, and, generally, become AP advocates in their school and community.
7. Advocates claim the presence of an AP course necessarily will strengthen and refocus the academic rigor of curriculum in the regular high school courses which lead to it, so even students who might not ascend to an AP course benefit.

While the Advanced Placement program clearly is the largest and, some might say, most successful program of its kind, it is not without its limitations or critics.

1. Despite the widespread recognition and acceptance of AP scores, students still experience a considerable meas-

ure of uncertainty about exactly how any particular college might regard the AP experience. A score accepted by one institute is no guarantee of acceptance by a second.

2. Because the AP score is determined by a uniform nation-wide exam administered each May, a tremendous premium is placed on one day's performance. A student who is ill, under personal stress, or simply not up to par on test day can see a year's worth of work result in no award of college credit.

3. By its own claim, the AP program is not intended for the average student. The intensity of the intellectual demands made upon students and even teachers necessarily limit the nature of the student body likely to benefit by participating. While it is true that heroic efforts by students and teachers sometimes can bring nontraditional students to levels of outstanding performance—see, for example, the work of Jaime Escalante (Quality Education for Minorities Project 1990, p. 68)—the AP program has remained the arena for a small percentage of any high school's student body: the very highest performing students. By providing excellence for a relatively few elite students within a high school, the AP program might deflect a general reexamination of the academic power and structure of a school. Such reexamination could result in a broader strengthening of the entire academic program for students of all abilities including the intellectually advanced, perhaps making AP courses superfluous (Sizer).

Syracuse University's Project Advance program. Syracuse University's Project Advance (SUPA),* founded in 1973, resulted from inquiries from several school districts in the Syracuse, N.Y., area to the university's vice chancellor for academic affairs. The school districts sought help in dealing with the problem of "senioritis."

Franklin P. Wilbur, one of the developers and the current director of Project Advance, describes SUPA as "the largest program in the country offering accredited college courses taught in the high schools by high school faculty" (1984, p. 45).

*Syracuse University Project Advance; 111 Waverly Ave., Syracuse, NY 13244-2320; (315) 423-2404.

After its local initiation in the Syracuse area, the program has grown to serve more than 75 high schools and approximately 4,000 students each year in New York, Massachusetts, Michigan, and New Jersey.

In SUPA, regular high school staff receive summer training at Syracuse University and teach the courses offered on their own high school campuses. The curriculum, which currently includes biology, calculus, chemistry, English, psychology, sociology, and computer engineering, mirrors the content of counterpart courses taught to Syracuse University students on the college campus. The courses have been adapted by joint college and high school teams to reflect the needs of high school students. Additionally, the courses, equivalent to three-credit semester courses at the college, are attenuated over the entire high school senior year. For these reasons, SUPA may be seen as a fusion of conceptual models 3h and 4h cited earlier.

After successfully completing the course work, take a test designed by the university's Center for Instructional Development with input from college and school personnel. Students receive high school credit for the course as well as college credit from the university.

If the student attends Syracuse University, the course is accepted in lieu of the same course on the college campus, and credit is granted. If the student chooses to attend another college or university, Syracuse issues an official transcript to that institution which then may evaluate the course as it would any transfer credit.

The credits earned by students seem quite portable, partly due, no doubt, to the reputation of Syracuse University. Wilbur and LaFay reported on a three-year study of SUPA students who sought to transfer SUPA credit to other institutions (1978, pp. 27-29). In 76 percent of all cases studied, students received credit for and exemption from college courses, and in 15 percent of the cases, students received credit but not exemption for college courses.

The profile of SUPA students indicates that their performance is superior to that of their peers who plan to attend college nationally. For example, the latest data available showed that SUPA students averaged nearly 100 points higher than the national mean on the verbal portion of the SAT and 117 points higher on the math section.

While 66.6 percent of SUPA students ranked in the top fifth

of their class, only 42.4 percent of students in the national sample made such a claim. Finally, whereas 41 percent of students nationally scored over 500 on the math SAT and 27 percent scored over 500 on the verbal SAT, SUPA students scored over 500 in math in 84.1 percent of the cases and in 60.1 percent of the cases.

In addition to the previously outlined general advantages of participating in college-level study, the SUPA model has several unique strengths:

1. Although students must take uniform final exams designed with input from high school faculty, the award of credit is based on a full year's work, giving teachers many opportunities to evaluate student learning.
2. Because the high school teachers must be appointed as Syracuse University adjuncts, they must be approved by the university's academic departments based on education, experience, and recommendation. This requirement, coupled with mandatory, specialized staff development conducted by the university, helps assure high standards in staffing and comparability to college curricular.
3. Although equal in every respect to college freshman courses, the SUPA courses are more accessible to high school seniors by their attenuation over a year-long period. This permits about twice the actual student-faculty contact hours than ordinarily possible when the same courses are taught to college freshmen, even though the same number of credits are awarded.
4. As with high school teachers involved in the AP program, the SUPA high school teachers are part of a collegial group of fellow practitioners who share goals, aspirations, techniques, and curriculum to the benefit of each other, their students, schools, and communities.

Although it's a program of high quality, SUPA nonetheless has a few limitations:

1. Although acceptance of the SUPA credits reportedly is high, acceptance isn't guaranteed except at Syracuse University.
2. Affiliated with a private university, the SUPA program charges tuition at a reduced rate. While financial aid might be available in special cases, some students might be discouraged by the tuition factor.
3. While reaching a somewhat broader range of students than

the AP program, SUPA has attracted, once again, a relatively rarefied segment of each participating high school's population. SUPA student profiles indicate that many average students do not participate in the SUPA program in schools in which it is offered.

Kingsborough Community College of the City University of New York's College Now program. Kingsborough Community College's College Now* is typical of a whole class of articulated programs that attempt to bring college study to high school classrooms. Under the auspices of these programs, specially selected and trained high school personnel as adjunct faculty teach college courses for the sponsoring postsecondary institution (Greenberg 1989, pp. 27–29). Syracuse University's Project Advance is another example of this program design (4h). Since College Now's target population is so markedly different, the program warrants separate discussion.

Begun in fall 1984, the College Now program works along the same lines as Syracuse University's Project Advance. In conjunction with eight New York City public high schools, Kingsborough approves faculty at each of the high schools to teach preselected college courses on the high school campuses.

Typical courses offered through College Now are humanities and introductions to business administration and basic, social, and computer sciences. Satisfactory completion results in high school and college credit. Remedial courses in writing and math also are offered, but without the promise of college credit.

Students in College Now receive special counseling services from college counselors who visit the high school each week. Also, each student is given the opportunity to visit the Kingsborough campus at least once each semester; students also are encouraged to explore the campus on their own and in guided groups.

The program seeks students who are moderate achievers—those students who have cumulative high school averages ranging between 65 percent and 80 percent. Serving this population is consistent with Kingsborough's mission as a community college.

*College Now, Kingsborough Community College, 2001 Oriental Blvd., Brooklyn, NY 11235; (718) 934-5170.

. . . Kingsborough approves faculty at each of the high schools to teach preselected college courses on the high school campuses.

In order to be placed in the tuition-free courses, students must complete a battery of CUNY-designed tests known collectively as the Freshman Assessment Program, which indicate levels of math, reading, and English competency. Those who score above the CUNY-prescribed mark are admitted, after counseling by college counselors who visit the high schools, to credit-bearing courses. Students who fall in the remedial range of the test results are invited to participate in the remedial course offerings. These students are promised that if they do participate and pass, they will receive the opportunity to take college-level courses the following semester.

The College Now program as implemented by Kingsborough Community College demonstrates several strong points. Chief among these:

1. The program is relatively successful for its intended low- and moderate-achieving population. In a recent year, for example, the 319 students enrolled had earned a cumulative grade average of slightly under B– in their College Now courses taken for college credit, exclusive of remedial courses. All considered, the College Now students passed 667 of the 959 credits for which they registered—a passing rate of 68.19 percent.

2. Recognizing the needs of its student body, College Now provides extra counseling support and makes effective motivational use of campus visits.

3. Using local high school faculty as Kingsborough adjuncts for the College Now program gives the program the benefit of an instructional staff that knows and understands the learning needs of the students, which serves as a critical point when dealing with a nontraditional population.

4. An unusual feature of the College Now program is its remedial component. Most programs of college-level placement insist on fairly rigorous entry criteria. As it provides college courses to the more able of the population, College Now also provides a remedial component for less able students. Therefore, those students not only receive the opportunity to improve their basic skills, but also the promise of college courses.

5. The College Now program staff is quite skilled at anticipating the administrative needs of the high schools that mount the program. The staff spends extensive amounts of time on the campuses working with key personnel to

fit the testing program, counseling sessions, and other College Now events into the complex schedules of the participating high schools.

6. In addition to the obvious motivational aspects to the involved students, principals of the participating high schools report that their respective communities highly appreciate and value the College Now program.

College Now is not without its limitations. Most significant among these are the following:

1. While one of the program's strengths and a large factor in its acceptance by high schools is its savvy administrative support staff, only extra funding from the state legislature makes possible such support. If this funding is unavailable, the program might suffer.

2. As with any program that depends upon a local institution as a credentialing agency, the college credits earned by students in the program are transferrable only to the extent that other colleges are willing to recognize those credits. As a relatively new program, the transfer experience is not yet well established.

State-sponsored concurrent-enrollment initiatives

Minnesota's Postsecondary Enrollment Options Program. The Postsecondary Enrollment Options Program (PSEOP),* proposed by the Minnesota legislature as part of the 1985 Omnibus School Aids Act, permitted high school juniors and seniors to take regular courses at colleges while receiving simultaneous high school and college credit without a charge for college tuition (Minnesota 1985 Omnibus School Aids Act). In both its original and current format, courses are taught by regular college faculty; therefore, the program is categorized as model 2c in the preceding table.

While the program has appealed to students and parents, it was not implemented without raising the ire of local school officials and teacher organizations. The opposition stemmed from the fact that in its original form, PSEOP reduced state aid to individual school districts by the amount of college tuition paid for every student who participated in the program.

*Commissioner of Education, Minnesota Department of Education, Capitol Square Building, 550 Cedar St., St. Paul, MN 55101.

High school students who elected to participate did so frequently only after encountering resistance from high school staff who viewed enrollment as a "brain drain" of better students to the college campuses. In addition, high school personnel were aware of the economic threat to their school districts—in the form of reduced state aid.

Of the 120,000 eleventh and twelfth graders in Minnesota, 1.5 percent participated in the program during the winter quarter of 1985, which was the first quarter the option was available. The rate of participation increased to 3.7 percent during the spring quarter, more than doubling the number of students enrolled (Randall 1986, p. 14).

The legislation that created the Postsecondary Enrollment Options Act called for an annual reduction of state school aid to local districts equaling the amount of the college tuition paid by the state to colleges for students from those districts who had enrolled under the plan. Therefore, several districts found themselves at the last quarterly disbursement period of the school year overexpended with respect to actual versus anticipated state aid. This consequence stemmed from the fact that the districts could not anticipate the level of student participation in the new program when school budgets were passed (prior to program initiation).

Fiscal ramifications aside, it is interesting to note that the first two groups of students in winter and spring fared as well as or better than their freshman counterparts in the same classes. According to a study conducted by the University of Minnesota, 31 percent of the high school students received grades of A, and 60 percent received grades of A or B (Randall 1986, p. 15).

Because of the obvious fiscal problems associated with the initial implementation of PSEOP, the program was modified by the legislature in 1986. The major changes included limiting to no more than the equivalent of two years of college credit students could earn, not permitting simultaneous high school and college credit awards for the college courses taken and passed, and if courses were taken for college credit, obligating the student to pay college tuition, although the state would pay tuition to colleges for college courses taken for high school credit.

No state-mandated entry criteria exist for admission into the program. Instead, students must meet the regular admissions standards applied by any particular institution.

The chief strength of the Postsecondary Enrollment Options Program is this: Many of Minnesota's rural school districts and high schools are quite small despite state pressures to consolidate them. It often is extremely difficult and costly for such schools to run high-powered advanced electives due to the relatively small pool of students available. For such districts, the availability of college-level study at local or regional postsecondary institutions permits advanced students with specialized interests to be served in ways not otherwise practical.

The main limitations of the Postsecondary Enrollment Options Program include the following:

1. Since students may not elect to take courses for simultaneous high school and college credit unless they plan to attend the sponsoring college after high school graduation, some of the benefits of a true concurrent-enrollment design might be vitiated somewhat. In particular, some of the acceleration possibilities necessarily are more limited.

2. The requirement that students must pay their own tuition if courses are taken for college credit might have a chilling effect on the ability of low-income students to participate in PSEOP, unless other arrangements for financial aid can be made.

3. In instances in which even the nearest college campus might be a very great distance from the high school, travel logistics simply can become unmanageable. Without alternative means of program delivery (tele-teaching, for example), students might be precluded from participation.

The Florida Model. In Florida, all state-funded colleges have been required by legislature to develop a plan with local school districts which would allow high school students concurrently to enroll in college courses. The courses must be held on high school campuses except in those cases in which technical facilities are available only on the college campus or when fewer than 15 high school students wish to be enrolled in a specific class (Florida Administrative Code 1983). Consequently, the Florida Dual-Enrollment Program represents several possible models: 2h, 2c, 4h, and 4c.

A typical agreement between a college and a local board of education would include sections that address procedures on how and where to provide courses, criteria to identify students, the courses to be offered, coordination of the college courses with the high school curriculum, and assurances that the college credit will transfer and that high school credit will be awarded. A typical agreement also would include guide-lines to inform students and parents about courses and proce-dures for application, information about relationships relating to administrative and procedural responsibilities, and pro-visions for coordinating courses, counseling services, instruc-tors, and equitable distribution of revenue (Seminole County School Board and Seminole Community College* 1986, pp. 1-11).

The manner in which the revenues are distributed equitably is interesting. Both the college and the school board may claim a concurrently enrolled student toward their respective full-time equivalent student membership. This differs from the Minnesota plan discussed previously.

High school faculty who teach college courses during the regular high school day are not paid additional salary; how-ever, the school district may charge the college at the regular college adjunct rate for allowing the college the privilege of utilizing school board staff to teach the college course. High school teachers who teach college courses after regular school hours receive additional compensation from the college.

College credits earned by the high school students are "banked" for them by the college until the students present evidence of high school graduation.

The program has been so successful that many secondary school and college administrators believe that the dual-enrollment program rapidly is replacing Advanced Placement in public high schools—largely by student demand.

Student population can vary markedly from school district to district and from community college to community college, since in every case the entry criteria are determined through negotiations between the colleges and the school districts. Interestingly, it is not unusual for a single community college to have negotiated several distinctly different agreements with different boards of education in its locality.

Florida's dual-enrollment program features many strengths:
1. The state's greatly flexible approach to concurrent enrollment is its chief strength. The dual-enrollment program
   is based on the wisdom that local parties, compelled by
   legislative edict, will negotiate out of a shared sense of

*Dr. Roger L. Jarand, Dean of Instructional Services, Seminole Community College, Sanford, FL 32771; (305) 323-1450.

self-interest; therefore, the program has assumed many varied configurations. Local educators have been able to address local needs with a real knowledge of those needs and the resources available to address them.

2. By making the state's community college system the focal point for its dual-enrollment efforts, Florida has sent a signal to students, parents, and school administrators that this is a program designed to be accessible, even to those who traditionally are excluded from participating in joint-enrollment programs.

As with all designs, some limitations exist. Perhaps somewhat incongruously, the program's greatest strength also might give rise to some serious flaws. Agreements between local school boards and community colleges must be negotiated. Therefore, the strength of a program depends at least in part on the willingness and ability of two complex institutions to agree, resulting in a quality program for students. A lack of understanding, personality variables, or sharply differing views of institutional missions might render negotiations less than successful.

Middle colleges, early colleges, and two-plus-two programs

While most of the efforts at concurrent enrollment have been aimed at developing programs that largely respect the 12 + 4 relationship between school systems and colleges, a few models have attempted to alter this structure by creating institutions which themselves straddle the traditional gap between high schools and colleges. One such structural innovation is described here.

Two-Plus-Two programs, strongly advocated by Dale Parnell in *The Neglected Majority* (1985, pp. 133-168), support concurrent high school and community/junior college credit but also call for significantly closer coordination of curriculum and instruction in vocational and technical areas (Shapiro 1986, p. 95). A prominent example of this broadly expanding movement is highlighted as well.

LaGuardia Community College's Middle College High School. Middle College High School,* a New York City Board

*Middle College, LaGuardia Community College, 31-10 Thomson Ave., Long Island City, NY 11101; (718) 482-5049.

of Education alternative high school located on the campus of LaGuardia Community College in Queens, N.Y., attempts to provide curricular continuity and emotional and developmental support to high school learners in college courses. The Middle College approach to simultaneous enrollment attempts to capitalize on easy access to the campus and curricular goals shared by Middle College and the cooperating college.

The school's curriculum is intended to meet the needs and motivate high-risk students who possess average potential.

Middle College students can take regular or special college courses at the college campus for simultaneous high school and college credit. Graduating seniors also can enroll in special courses taught for high school credit by college faculty. These special courses are available to juniors or seniors with good records at Middle College, students who have completed a sequence of high school courses in an area and now need to take the next course in the sequence, or students who want to do advanced work in which they have special talent or skill (Lieberman 1986, pp. 13-14).

Middle College represents several models of concurrent enrollment, including 1h, 1c, 2h, 2c, 4h, and 4c.

Students who desire to take college classes must see one of the Middle College counselors and be interviewed to determine eligibility. That same counselor will monitor the student's progress periodically during the college experience.

On average, 90 Middle College students take college courses each year, earning from 1 credit to 15 credits. Since Middle College opened in 1974, some 700 students or 30 percent of the population have taken and completed college courses.

Historically, Middle College students have earned two-thirds of the college credits for which they have registered, maintaining a mean grade-point average in those classes of slightly under C+.

Admission to Middle College requires students to graduate from one of six local junior high schools and to have exhibited the following behavior in junior high: (1) a high rate of absenteeism; (2) three or more subject-area failures; (3) identified social and emotional problems stemming from the home environment; and (4) evidence of some potential to successfully engage, initially, in high school-level work (Lieberman 1986, p. 3).

All Middle College students have been identified as potential high school dropouts by their junior high school teachers and counselors.

According to the most recent data, approximately 53 percent of Middle College students are more than two years behind level in reading and 40 percent are more than two years behind level in math. The ethnic distribution of the student body is roughly 45 percent white, 33 percent Hispanic, 21 percent black, and 1 percent Asian. About 60 percent of the approximately 500 students are on public assistance (Cullen and Moed 1988, p. 41).

The typical Middle College student who takes college courses while in high school has a high school average between 70 percent and 80 percent, SAT verbal scores in the 300 to 350 range, and SAT math scores in the 350 to 400 range.

The Middle College model has many strengths:

1. The Middle College design makes great use of the phenomenon known as the "power of the site." By placing high school students in a college environment, they have a chance to observe college students modeling appropriate, mature behavior.
2. Being on the college campus allows faculty from both the college and the high school to work together on curricular continuity. This shared process is enhanced by the fact that many Middle College teachers are employed by the college as adjuncts to teach college classes to the regular college population. College personnel frequently teach special college or high school classes for the Middle College students.
3. Middle College students who enroll in college classes receive the benefit of counseling, advising, and tutoring from both the high school and the college, thereby increasing, especially for the marginal student, chances for success.
4. Because both Middle College and LaGuardia prominently feature cooperative education in their curricular designs, unique opportunity exists for Middle College students to earn college coop credit while in high school, in addition to the more traditional areas of college study.

The model also has a few limitations:

1. While both the Middle College and LaGuardia staffs have

worked well together over the years, significant cultural differences between the institutions still are evident, although most of the time these differences do not appear to get in the way. Contractual divergence, separate pay scales, differing calendars, and even dissimilar holidays all must be handled with sensitivity by college and high school leadership, lest the cooperative spirit be diminished. In the cases of many other concurrent-enrollment programs, the actual physical distance between school and college campuses and faculties helps to deemphasize these contrasts. In the Middle College model, we see almost daily reminders.

2. As with all cases of collaboration between schools and community colleges, the transferability of the college credits earned by the high school students almost is dependent totally upon the quality of the articulation arrangements that have been made between the community college and senior colleges.

Virginia's The Master Technician Program. The Master Technician Program* has been developed with the support of Virginia's governor and the cooperation of the Virginia State Board of Education and the Virginia State Community College System. Significant local institutions and groups included Thomas Nelson Community College, the New Horizons Technical Center, and the school systems of Hampton, Newport News, Poquoson, Williamsburg/James City County, and York County (Wimmer 1988, p. 96). Implemented in fall 1986 after a two-year planning period, it is a primary example of the "Two-Plus-Two" model, as espoused by Parnell:

> *Beginning with the junior year in high school, students will select the tech-prep program . . . and continue for four years in a structured and closely coordinated curriculum. They will be taught by high school teachers in the first two years but will also have access to college personnel and facilities when appropriate. . . . [T]he high-school portion of the career program will be intentionally preparatory in nature. Built around career clusters and technical-systems study, such a tech-prep approach will help students develop broad-based competence in a career field and avoid the pitfalls of . . . narrowly delineated job training (1985, p. 144).*

*Linda Schiflette, Assistant Director for Vocational Education, Hampton City Schools, 1819 Nicholson Blvd., Hampton, VA 23663; (804) 850-5392.

The program has many interesting features including a reduction in course redundancy which allows for greater concentrations in college prep or technical specialization. It also includes great student career-path flexibility that permits options after the A.A.S. to enter the employment market, pursue higher education vertically for a B.S. in the same field, or move laterally into another baccalaureate area of study. Finally, a broad mix of academic and vocational options are offered at both the secondary and postsecondary levels; business, industry, and government courses collaborate to assure technical education is relevant to the work world (Wimmer 1988).

ENRICHMENT, COMPENSATORY, AND MOTIVATIONAL PARTNERSHIP MODELS

The distinction between the models and programs discussed in Section 5 and those in this chapter is that enrichment, compensatory, and motivational partnerships are not designed with concurrent enrollment as their primary thrust. While in some cases a concurrent-enrollment component might be included in a larger programmatic package, the major emphases of these models are to enrich the secondary school experience, assist students in developing basic and more advanced skills, or provide inspiration, motivation, and support for students who otherwise might not consider seriously the college option after completing high school.

What are Enrichment, Compensatory, And Motivational Partnership Models?

To illustrate this discussion, enrichment, compensatory, and motivational models are described as independent, free-standing approaches. In reality it often is difficult to disenbraid them. Their goals, target populations, and programmatic approaches often overlap and typically are mutually supportive. Through partnerships between high schools and colleges, enrichment programs are designed to provide curricular, cocurricular, and extracurricular experiences which would not otherwise be available to the high school students for whom they are intended.

Compensatory partnership designs give students opportunities to improve their basic skills—reading, writing, math, and spoken language—while also often encouraging pursuit of other skills such as study and library skills which might aid them in both high school and college work. Compensatory partnerships often differ from traditional secondary offering areas: They might stress new technology or research; they jointly are developed by college and high school faculty; they might make use of special funding, facilities, or equipment available through the college; and they often involve early identification and intervention.

Motivational partnerships, while offering encompassing enrichment and compensatory elements, focus on encouraging students to complete high school, take appropriate college-preparatory curricula, and seriously consider college after high school as part of a comprehensive review of career planning options.

Why Are These Partnership Models Important?

As discussed in Section 5, a continuing interest is focused on students whose needs might not be well served in high schools. Enrichment programs respond to the fact that without special facilities, curricula, and faculty, it often is impossible for individual, traditionally structured schools to provide the kind of intellectual stimulation some students—especially the gifted—require. The Johns Hopkins University Center for the Advancement of Academically Talented Youth—which will be described more fully later—is one of the earliest and most successful efforts in the enrichment field. Typically, the program embraces as its rationale the desire to provide talented youngsters with an individualized, naturally sequenced curriculum related to students' abilities and notwithstanding their often precocious age (Durden 1985, p. 38).

Partnerships in which the primary focuses are compensatory and motivational often focus on the needs of underrepresented, minority, and at-risk populations. An eloquent rationale for action was stated by the Quality Education for Minorities Project (1990, pp. 11-13):

> *Many schools, including those with predominantly minority student bodies, continue to operate with outmoded curricula and structures based on the assumption that only a small elite will have or need to have substantial academic success. The problems [Alaska Native, Native American, black, and Hispanic] children face in and out of the classroom—racism, poverty, language differences, and cultural barriers—are not adequately addressed in today's typical school. We have had, consequently, low achievement and high dropout rates. . . . It is in the schools, the increasingly minority schools, that the economic future of the United States will be determined. . . . The economic and demographic changes facing our country make a quality education—education that works—essential for all of us* (1990, p. 11-13).

The Benefits of Enrichment, Compensatory, And Motivational Partnerships

Taken together or singly, high school-college partnerships that provide enrichment, compensatory skills, and/or motivation benefit students, parents, institutions, and society, mirroring the advantages of dual-enrollment programs discussed in Section 5. For students, these programs are a source of motivation, enhanced skills development, and an enriched and extended curriculum.

For parents, the benefits include a heightened sense of their own role in their children's higher education opportunities, a more complete sense of the resources available to them and their children, and a clearer, often affirmative understanding of their children's potential to succeed in a postsecondary environment.

For high schools, partnerships can hold several attractions. Assistance in basic skills development might allow youngsters to move from very expensive remedial programs to lower cost general education classes. Students who are motivated to complete school might make fewer demands on a school's guidance and disciplinary team. Increased skills and motivation can result in better test results on standardized tests, better attendance, and higher retention rates, all of which might improve the school's standing with colleges and regional and state accrediting agencies. Furthermore, these programs can be very helpful in making the senior year more enjoyable, productive, and meaningful, alleviating dreaded "senioritis." Interaction with colleges also can provide boons to staff development and community relations.

[Partnerships] are difficult to establish, difficult to sustain [and] require significant leaps of trust and faith. . . .

Colleges might seek partnerships not only because they're aware of new grant-seeking opportunities, but also because well-founded hope exists that innovative remedial efforts in high school can reduce the need for remediation in college. Simultaneously, student time and money is saved, and colleges are spared the expense of providing the remediation (Suss and Goldsmith 1989, p. 114). One such major effort in this area is illustrated by Prefreshman Summer Program at the City University of New York, for example. Initiated in 1985, the program serves more than 7,000 prefreshmen each summer. At-risk students are targeted for basic skills instruction, tutoring, group and individual counseling and advising, career workshops, and study skills, in addition to traditional freshman orientation activities. The program, now offered on all 17 undergraduate campuses of the university, appears to be quite successful: Student participants demonstrate retention rates 20 percent higher through the sophomore year when compared to comparably skilled students who had not participated ("Prefreshman Summer Immersion" 1989, p. 5).

Additionally, colleges might benefit by recruiting better prepared, more highly motivated students than otherwise possible, and enjoy the opportunity to provide significant pre-admissions services (Phillips 1987, p. 13). Colleges also benefit from an increased awareness of current high school curricula and instructional practices, a better sense of the levels of student preparedness for college work, and insights into the attitudes of high school students regarding their interests and reasons for choosing—or not choosing—disciplines, careers, courses, and colleges. Finally, colleges can parlay their partnerships with high schools into more generalized, positive community relationships.

The possibility of improved recruitment opportunities often is raised as a good reason to engage in partnerships. I believe, however, that this reason might be oversold. My own observations as principal of the Middle College at LaGuardia Community College from 1976-1981 revealed that about 30 percent of a small graduating class of approximately 100 students continued on at LaGuardia. More recently, Cullen and Moed cite a LaGuardia entrance rate of 27 percent (1988, p. 48). Whether these numbers alone would justify the costs of partnerships to a college is questionable. The conclusion that might be drawn here is that while attracting additional students is certainly a possibility, the actual numbers of students who might be attracted by a partnership program might be small. A college should enter a partnership aware of this factor and harbor additional reasons for involvement, or risk disappointment.

Whether aimed at the gifted, those at risk, those of low income, minorities, or urban dwellers, some common themes for partnerships emerge: They are difficult to establish, difficult to sustain, require significant leaps of trust and faith, and, yet, they are seen by nearly all observers as an essential ingredient for successful schooling in the future. In a discussion of partnerships for urban schools, the Carnegie Foundation for the Advancement of Teaching expresses some seminal sentiments about the nature of all high school-college partnerships, no matter what their target populations:

The jurisdictional boundaries separating schools and colleges are crossed only when institutions on both sides of the line are amenable. It is not easy to build incentives for cooperation if one institution considers itself the winner and the other sees itself as the loser. In all of this, a special burden falls on higher education. The nation's colleges and uni-

*versities must, in tangible ways, affirm the essentialness of
the nation's urban schools. . . . Collaboration is not an auto-
matic virtue. Not every cooperative venture is destined for
success. But to those who make the effort and occasionally
succeed, the rewards are high and students well served.
There can be no better reason for working together* (1988,
p. 46).

Conceptual Models of Enrichment, Compensatory, And Motivational Partnerships

The defining characteristics of the high school-college partnerships discussed here may be distributed into three areas:
the chief programmatic goal, the primary target population,
and the service-delivery site. The chart below presents a
graphic representation of the interplay of these characteristics.

Models of Enrichment, Compensatory, and Motivational Partnerships

CHIEF PROGRAMMATIC GOAL

TARGET POPULATION	Enrichment	Compensatory	Motivational
Minority/At-Risk	1 h,c,h/c	2 h,c,h/c	3 h,c,h/c
Gifted	4 h,c,h/c	5 h,c,h/c	6 h,c,h/c
General	7 h,c,h/c	8 h,c,h/c	9 h,c,h/c

h = Service on high school campus
c = Service on college campus
h/c = Service on both high school and college campuses

Three chief programmatic goals are illustrated: enrichment,
compensatory, and motivational. Each of these thrusts previously has been defined. The primary target populations for
the partnerships have been grouped into three major categories: minority and/or at-risk students, gifted students, and
the general high school population. Finally, service delivery
may take place on the college campus, the high school campus, or on both the high school and college campuses.

As with any conceptual model, it is possible to locate an
occasional program that defines its target population somewhat differently (such as low income) or describes its primary
goal in somewhat different terms (career exploration, for
example). Nevertheless, even these terms may be subsumed
appropriately in the previous matrix.

It also is very likely that a single program might be assigned

---

to several different cells of the model. For example, a partnership might target minority/at-risk and general students for motivational and compensatory treatments which include remedial courses at the high school and college campus visits, thus falling into cells 2h, 3c, 8h, and 9c.

Examples of Enrichment, Compensatory, And Motivational Partnerships

Because so many partnerships have overlapping goals, populations and service locations, no attempt is made here to present a "typical" model based on any of these parameters. Rather, a more eclectic approach has been selected through which well-documented, successful, and important partnership efforts are presented with the model types noted.

The University of California-Berkeley's MESA program

One of the oldest and most successful partnership programs is UC-Berkeley's original Mathematics, Engineering, Science Achievement program (MESA),* begun in 1970, which has expanded to 16 college and university centers. It involves 100 to 400 students at each site (Wilbur, Lambert, and Young 1987, p. 39). The program is targeted at minority high school students, particularly blacks and Mexican-Americans. The original Berkeley program featured academic advisement, summer enrichment programs, scholar incentive awards, career advising and college advising (Smith, 1985, pp. 20-21). Other program features include study groups, tutoring, and field trips.

The program focuses on all three major goals: enrichment, compensation, and motivation. The majority of services are delivered on the high school campuses, but significant events also take place on the college campus (Broatch 1989). The partnership, therefore, can be identified as several model types, including 1h/c, 2h, and 3h/c.

According to Smith, MESA's success may be judged by its expansion to 16 California university centers with more than 4,000 students from 140 secondary schools (1985, p. 24). Approximately 90 percent of MESA graduates enter college, and more than 60 percent are accepted into a math-related college major.

Some questions have been raised about the program's out-

*University of California–Berkeley, Lawrence Hall of Science, Level D, Berkeley, CA 94720; (213) 743-2127.

comes and policy decision-making process in the California legislature, however. The program recently has begun to shift efforts to earlier intervention, raising in some minds the propriety of university-school system ventures in which the university seemingly takes over a public school system (California State Postsecondary School Commission 1989).

Ohio State University's Early College Mathematics Placement Testing program

In 1977, the EMPT program* was initiated at Westlake High School near Columbus, Ohio, and since has grown to encompass dozens of other schools. The program conceptually is simple and remarkably effective. Local high schools agree to administer to college-bound juniors the university's mathematics placement exam, usually given to entering OSU freshmen during the summer orientation program. Individual test results are mailed to students by the university. Summary reports are mailed to the high schools, which have agreed to provide appropriate guidance services and courses to meet student needs.

Students who find that they are deficient in math either can take additional college-preparatory courses or remedial courses (as indicated by exam results) prior to high school graduation.

As a result of the testing and guidance program, a significant increase has been noted in the number of high school seniors who take math courses; a decrease has been noted in the number of students who take remedial math as college freshmen at OSU (Brizius and Cooper 1984).

The program exemplifies models 8h and 9h.

Colorado Community College's Partners Program

The Colorado Community College and Occupational Education System with Denver Public Schools and the Colorado Minority Engineering Association has created the Partners Program,† located at the Community College of Denver.

*The Ohio Early College Mathematics Placement Testing Program (EMPT), Ohio State University, 100 Math Building, 231 West 18th Ave., Columbus, OH 43210-1101; (614) 292-0694.

†Partnerships Program, Colorado Community College, Campus Box 203, P.O. Box 173363, Denver, CO 80217-3363; (303) 556-2600.

Targeted at minorities with special focus on black, Hispanic and American Indian students, the program's goal is to motivate students to graduate from high school and to consider college career paths. The program provides support to both students and their parents in a variety of forms. Among the major activities are visits to the CCD campus and other colleges, meetings with college financial aid counselors, presentations by business leaders and a summer college-preparation program sponsored by CCD and held on its campus (Raughton, et al, 1989).

The Partners Program exemplifies models 2c and 3c.

The Center for the Advancement of Academically Talented Youth (CTY) at Johns Hopkins University

Begun in 1971 as an experiment and formalized as part of the university's operating structure in 1979, CTY* is perhaps one of the oldest and best researched programs of its kind (Durden 1985, pp. 39, 41). Screening is limited to those students who score above the 97th percentile on nationally normed standardized tests of verbal and mathematical ability. These students, in turn, take the Scholastic Aptitude Test: Roughly one-third of these students qualify for the program (Wilbur, Lambert, and Young 1987, p. 51).

In addition to Johns Hopkins, regional college and university sites around the country are used to provide advanced academic study for winter, summer, residential, and commuter programs. A mail course in expository writing is offered as well. Grades are not issued in courses; rather, a descriptive summary of each student's progress is reported to sending schools. In addition to direct instruction, the program offers other services, including:

> *Assessment and evaluation; . . . counseling; a training institute for educators and parents; career education workshops; . . . and a pilot skill reinforcement program for educationally and economically disadvantaged youth (Wilbur, Lambert, and Young 1987, p. 51).*

Chiefly through college campus-based interventions, the program addresses the needs of the gifted for enrichment and motivational activities. To a lesser degree, it also addresses

---

*Center for the Advancement of Academically Talented Youth, The Johns Hopkins University, Charles and 34th sts., Baltimore, MD 21218; (301) 338-8427.

these same needs and those of basic skills reinforcement for disadvantaged students. CTY may be classified as models 1c, 2c, 3c, 4c, and 6c.

Miami-Dade Community College's
Partners in Education program

Initiated in 1987 in partnership with the Dade County Public Schools, Partners in Education* targets black high school students. The program is a comprehensive model designed to identify students early in their high school careers and support them until they earn their high school diploma, an associate of arts degree from Miami-Dade, and a bachelor's degree from a senior college. The program focuses on "academic preparation, career planning, positive reference group expectancy, and institutional and financial support" (Phillips 1987, p. 11). College faculty work with high school teachers to design remedial courses, improve information systems, and design support programs. Funding provides financial incentives and rewards for students—the amounts vary based upon grades earned in each high school course. A similar structure supports students when they attend Miami-Dade.

The program exemplifies models 1h/c, 2h, and 3h/c.

*Partners in Education Opportunity Program, Miami-Dade Community College, 300 N.E. 2nd Ave., Miami, FL 33132; (305) 237-3540.

ACADEMIC ALLIANCES AND OTHER
TEACHER-TO-TEACHER PARTNERSHIPS

Partnerships that focus on college faculty who work closely
with secondary school teachers on matters of common curricular or pedagogical concern acknowledge the primacy of
classroom teachers in the teaching-learning process and their
importance as change agents in any attempt to restructure
public education (Boyer 1984, p. 526).

What are Academic Alliances and Other
Teacher-to-Teacher Partnerships?

All of the programs described in this section have at least four
characteristics in common. First, they involve secondary
school teachers who already practice in the schools, so they
differ from traditional preservice teacher-training efforts
(Gross 1988, pp. 10-15). Second, the programs join college
faculty—often from academic disciplines rather than schools
of education—with high school teachers to work collaboratively on an agenda (Bagasao 1990, p. 6). Third, because the
projects are ambitious and because it takes time to develop
close relationships between high school teachers and college
faculty, the programs typically are of long duration as opposed
to the more typical one-shot, expert consultations (Gray 1985,
p. 61) or college faculty guest lectures (Gaudiani 1985, pp.
71, 77; Vivian 1985b, p. 88). Fourth, these programs generally
share the goal of professional development.

Why Are These Partnerships Important?

Practitioners for many years have recognized some of the
incongruities confronting teachers. Claire Gaudiani describes
rather succinctly two of the major paradoxes:

> *Paradox No. 1: Those who spend the most time developing
> our children's minds are not encouraged to develop their
> own. Paradox No. 2: College faculty are not expected, how-
> ever, to share [their] knowledge on a regular basis with
> school teachers who teach classes in the very same subject
> in the very same town* (1985, pp. 69-70).

One basis for the desirability of this kind of college-high
school faculty interchange might stem in part from the belief
that the intellectual abilities of public school teachers might
be open to some doubt. For example, in comparing the math-

ematics and verbal Scholastic Aptitude Test scores for all college-bound seniors with those who intended to major in education for the years 1973 through 1985, the Carnegie Forum on Education and the Economy found that students who desired to enter teaching had scored substantially lower than average and that nearly half of these students came from high schools without college-preparatory programs (1986, pp. 29, 32).

In addition to the questions raised about the intellectual ability of school teachers, those teachers taken as a group who work in the schools have been doing so much longer than their counterparts of just a few years ago. Older, more experienced teachers have invaluable insights to share, but with whom can they share them? All those years in the classroom can lead to "burn out" and increased levels of job dissatisfaction. What's more, the years away from undergraduate and graduate school experiences might leave teachers out of touch with the latest developments in their academic disciplines.

The ultimate importance of these partnerships stems from the belief that better prepared, more up-to-date teachers who have enjoyed opportunities for professional growth and fulfillment will serve their students better.

On the other hand, the long-range success of these partnerships ultimately may be determined by the ability of these alliances to respond to some significant issues. The majority of teacher-to-teacher partnerships and especially Academic Alliances have been initiated by colleges and universities rather than by secondary school teachers themselves. An inherent danger—one which would appear to have been addressed successfully so far in the cases reported here, at least—is the potential for high school teachers to feel patronized by their "betters." Obviously, great sensitivity to this concern must be exhibited by university faculty.

Another potential pitfall is the possibility that university personnel can come to dominate the alliances themselves out of the power implicit in their roles as conveners and experts. While a partnership might be able to operate for a period of time in this fashion, it is doubtful that it could be sustained successfully under such circumstances.

Finally, an important measure of the success of these partnerships might be their growth beyond the academic disciplines that tend to foster them. Most partnerships have been developed in areas in which the articulation needs are very pragmatic. It probably is not coincidental that the Academic Alliance movement began in the area of foreign language study. This area still, incidentally, continues to harbor the greatest number of such partnerships (Bagasao 1990, p. 6). Many partnerships have been established in writing and math, both of which traditionally are viewed as realms in which articulation is highly desirable—perhaps because of the developmental nature of these subjects. Sadly, however, the humanities (with the exception of the National Faculty program and some local efforts) have not been as fertile an area for partnerships. Do some elements exist within this subject (and the arts, for that matter) or within those involved in these fields which tends to mitigate successful partnerships? One would hope that alliances in these disciplines could be developed in greater number—if only because of the richness of the intellectual stimulation such interactions might produce.

Another potential pitfall is the possibility that university personnel can come to dominate the alliances themselves. . . .

The Benefits of Teacher-to-Teacher Partnerships

The benefits of teacher-to-teacher partnerships appear in many areas. For high school teachers these include a heightened sense of professionalism; improved self-esteem; increased knowledge of their academic discipline; heightened expectations for students; and an increased commitment to teaching careers.

The benefits to college faculty who participate in teacher-to-teacher programs have been discussed widely. These include a contemporary understanding of high school practice, an opportunity to make college contributions—which is important for tenure and promotion considerations—and the potential to conduct writing projects or research or prepare grant proposals, all of which can enhance the prestige and influence of a faculty member on campus and in the academic community as well.

High school students whose teachers take part in teacher-to-teacher programs also benefit. First, they are taught by teachers who are more highly motivated, better trained, armed with contemporary knowledge and techniques, and more committed than ever to their profession. Also, their teachers are very likely to expect better student performance. All of these factors can improve student learning (Vivian 1985b, p. 86).

Examples of Academic Alliances and Other Teacher-to-Teacher Partnerships

Academic Alliances

The Academic Alliances movement is one of the largest partnership forms studied here, with 350 alliances across the United States. In 1989, the John D. and Catherine T. MacArthur Foundation for the National Project in Support of Academic Alliances* provided aid to the American Association for Higher Education (Bagasao 1990, p.6). The current Academic Alliances program had its start in 1981 in foreign language study, and was supported by the several foundations. The original project was called "Strengthening the Humanities Through Foreign Language and Literature Studies" (Byrd 1985, pp. 65-68). Since that time, however, the movement has grown to "more than 350 alliances: 145 in foreign languages, more than 50 in physics, 26 in chemistry, 46 in geography, and more than 30 in history. Another 50 or so exist in mathematics and political science and in interdisciplinary areas such as humanities and social studies" (Bagasao 1990, p. 6).

Academic Alliances are an attempt to bring together high school teachers and college faculty who have a common curricular focus to discuss common interests and concerns (Gross 1988, pp. 15-17). Unlike most inservice programs offered to secondary school teachers, Academic Alliances are events dominated by teachers, rather than by supervisors (Gaudiani 1985, p. 70).

Alliances often begin as relatively informal activities; just two or three local faculty members form the group's core (Wilbur, Lambert, and Young 1987, p. 13). Alliances tend to hold monthly or bimonthly meetings and groups usually expand to include from 12 to 60 members with a preponderance of high school teachers (Gross 1988, p. 16). Meetings usually focus on professional development and improving teaching and learning (Bagasao 1990, p. 6). Activities might include reviews of literature and research, presentations, demonstration lessons, and reports of major conferences (Gaudiani 1985, pp. 71-72).

Gaudiani and Burnett stress the contributions both secondary and college teachers can make to the process, emphasiz-

---

*National Project in Support of Academic Alliances, American Association for Higher Education, One Dupont Circle, Washington, DC 20036; (202) 293-6440.

ing the commonalities of their disciplines (1986, p. 8).
Indeed, Gaudiani emphasizes the fundamental democracy
of the process, its teacher-talk centeredness, and the fact that
college personnel should not take exclusive responsibility
for planning the alliances' activities (1985, p. 72). Gross, while
acknowledging the success of Academic Alliances, regards
the emphasis on equality as somewhat defensive and asserts
that differences in college and high school cultures are both
necessary and healthy and should be acknowledged (1988,
p. 16).

Greater Boston Foreign Language Collaborative

An early example of an Academic Alliances program is the
Greater Boston Foreign Language Collaborative. Established
in 1984, it involves teachers from the public schools of Boston, Cambridge, Lexington, Newton, and Concord-Carlisle and
Wellesley high schools. College faculty are drawn from Boston
College, Boston University, Brandeis, Northeastern, Pine
Manor, and the University of Massachusetts, Boston. The goal
of the alliance is to provide a forum for foreign language
teachers to discuss common concerns and professional goals.
Special emphasis is placed on the continuity of curricula and
classroom practices.

The alliance supports two types of groups: forums and priority interest groups. Forums comprise teachers and faculty
from all levels; those groups concern themselves with topics
such as goals of instruction, curricular continuity, and providing smoother transitions for students from level to level.
Priority interest groups provide a more narrow field of attention often centered around specific activities or areas such
as foreign exchanges, technology and computers, and language proficiency. Interest groups, typically numbering
between 30 and 80 members, share their findings with the
forums.

The alliance is organized by a steering committee which
is co-chaired by one representative selected by the school
systems and high schools and a second by the colleges and
universities. Other members of the steering committee represent functional areas and responsibilities, again, with equal
college and secondary school representation (College Board
1987).

Cuyahoga Community College Collaborative with Cleveland, East Cleveland, and Lakewood public schools

Teacher-to-teacher programs often are ingredients in a larger recipe for school-college partnerships, as is the case with the Cuyahoga Community College Collaborative.* Project discussion began in 1983, and the collaborative formally was initiated in 1986. Its dual goals are to improve educational continuity for students and to enhance opportunities for school and college faculty. One of the major initial thrusts of the partnership was the formulation of the Urban Initiative Language Education Program, a computer-based writing project. Some of the spinoff activities from this are the development of supplemental curriculum units and teacher-to-teacher peer coaching.

Another significant activity has been the creation of "teacher dialogues." Focused on four academic areas (art, math, science, and English), college faculty and school teachers meet regularly to share ideas and experiences. The dialogues have, in turn, led to a series of more narrowly focused activities such as teacher workshops, which have maintained the school-college collaborative.

Each of the three school districts along with Cuyahoga Community College has appointed representatives to the joint steering committee, and each partner projects equal weight in planning and implementing all project activities. All told, the collaborative involves approximately 24,000 students, three-quarters of whom are members of ethnic minority groups. Some 370 high school teachers and 250 college faculty are involved in the project (College Board 1987).

National Writing Project

The National Writing Project† originated in 1974 as the Bay Area Writing Project, initiated by the University of California-

---

*Center for Articulation and Transfer Opportunities, Cuyahoga County Community College, 2900 Community College Ave., Cleveland, OH 44115; (216) 987-4044.

†The National Writing Project, Dr. James Gray, Director, 5627 Tolman Hall, School of Education, University of California-Berkeley, Berkeley, CA 94720; (415) 642-0963.

Berkeley in partnership with several local school districts. At the time, a strong sense prevailed that few teachers had been trained properly to teach writing—whether in college or in the secondary schools. Some educators and academics also believed that previous major efforts at improving the skills of writing teachers had been fairly unsuccessful in affecting actual practice in the classrooms, because these projects largely modeled the top-design nature of most inservice staff training models (Gray 1985, pp. 60-61).

The program's main objectives are to improve the standard of writing instruction, to provide an effective staff development model for the schools, to provide an effective model for university-school collaboration, and to extend the professional roles of classroom teachers.

The National Writing Project is, as its name implies, a national program. In implementation, however, sites develop due to local initiative and, typically, by funding from community or regional sources (although at times small amounts of seed money have been made available through the National Project). In some cases, state support has been made available to local partnerships (Gray 1985, p. 64).

The staff development program of the project is rigorous and highly structured, and the key responsibility for the model's success rests initially and ultimately on the responsiveness of classroom teachers to committing their talents, integrity, and creativity as well as their willingness to share and openly critique themselves and colleagues. Several components are regarded as key to a local project's successful adoption. These components include selecting the best writing teachers for the initial summer institute (Gray 1986, p. 9); using teacher demonstration lessons critiqued by peers; focusing on writing and including regular writing sessions by teachers; focusing on research about writing instruction; implementing sustained, multisession follow-up programs for teachers after the initial summer institute and extending throughout the school year; and encouraging an openness to new ideas and approaches (Gray 1985, pp. 65-68).

The project exists at more than 140 sites throughout the United States and includes several additional sites overseas. It has received support from several funding sources including the National Endowment for the Humanities, the Carnegie Corporation of New York, the University of California-Berkeley (Wilbur, Lambert, and Young 1987, p. 87), and the Andrew

W. Mellon Foundation (Gray 1985, p. 64).

Looking at a local site of the NWP offers insight into how the project's precepts can be put into action.

University Of Oregon's Oregon Writing Project

The Oregon Writing Project* began at the University of Oregon in 1978, identifying master teachers in the local public secondary schools. The teachers then attended four- to five-week summer intensive programs on the university campus. They, in turn, became "turnkey" teachers during the regular school year when they returned to their campuses and trained colleagues in the techniques they had learned. Interestingly, neither the identification of the master teachers nor the teachers later trained in the schools is limited to English teachers. Rather, the program includes volunteers from any academic discipline who are interested in improving the writing practice of themselves and their students. During the school year, the master teachers experience additional training and sharing.

The success of the university's efforts is attributable to two factors: using experienced, local teachers rather than outside experts and requiring teachers to spend a great deal of time actually engaged in writing (Wilbur, Lambert, and Young 1987, p. 87).

The National Faculty

The National Faculty,† originally called the National Humanities Faculty, is one of the largest and oldest collaborative programs. It was established in 1968 with a $6 million grant from the National Endowment for the Humanities (Gross 1988, p. 12). The National Faculty involves more than 700 humanists from higher education and takes a rather open-ended, responsive view of its role with schools. After local schools present proposals to the program, college professors are identified to work on the particular project at that site. Originally, faculty were not selected necessarily because of their geographic proximity to the localities; lately, however, this factor has been

*Oregon Writing Project, Department of English, University of Oregon, Eugene, OR 97403; (503) 686-3911.

†The National Faculty, 1676 Clifton Rd., Atlanta, GA 30322; (404) 727-5788.

a greater consideration to increase cost-effectiveness and allow a greater concentration of services on an institution-to-institution level (Maeroff 1983, pp. 34-36).

The goals of the project are to teach high school teachers more about their subject area, to allow them to enter into intellectual relationships with their peers, and to increase their effectiveness as classroom teachers (National Faculty 1987, p. 2). The typical process is a local plan of approximately two years' duration, including several visits by a college professor to plan a two- or three-week summer institute involving 30 to 40 participants, the summer institute itself, follow-up activities during the school year, and planning for the involvement of local colleges and universities to help sustain the project after its initial period (Gross 1988, p. 13).

This is a "slow change" model that depends upon prolonged involvement between the school and university personnel consistent with the recommendation of the Commission on the Humanities (1980, p. 56).

One of the more ambitious, sustained projects supported by the National Faculty has been with the Atlanta Public Schools.

Atlanta Public Schools Project with the National Faculty
Begun in 1983, this joint partnership has expanded to involve the high schools of the Atlanta Public Schools with the National Faculty.* The program draws upon the faculty resources of several area colleges and universities including Agnes Scott, Atlanta, Emory, Georgia State, Georgia Institute of Technology, and Spelman.

Major project activities include a university-led program of institutes which involves more than 200 high school teachers each summer. An additional 200 teachers participate in institutes held during the course of the regular school year. High school teachers also may write proposals to compete for mini-grants of $1,000 to initiate innovative programs in the humanities.

Additionally, the program supports the formation of working teams of high school and college staff, faculty collaboration with local and national humanities scholars, seminars and demonstration classes, and projects. All told, these activ-

*Atlanta Public Schools with The National Faculty, Project Director, The National Faculty, 1676 Clifton Rd., Atlanta, GA 30322; (404) 727-5788.

ities result in programmatic benefits to approximately 30,000 students each year, in the subject areas of English, history, foreign languages, and fine arts.

The Yale-New Haven Teachers Institute

One of the older partnerships, the Teachers Institute* jointly was established in 1978 by Yale University and the New Haven (Conn.) Public Schools (Wilbur, Lambert, and Young 1987, p. 13). The program was designed as a response to the belief that many teachers in the New Haven Public Schools were less than adequately prepared to teach their subjects, especially in science, math, and the humanities. In New Haven, specifically, only 58.8 percent of secondary teachers of humanities and 36 percent of the math and science teachers had majored as undergraduates or graduate students in the areas they taught (Vivian 1985b, pp. 79-80). Additionally, the very low teacher turnover rate in New Haven nearly assured that the majority of teachers had been in service for long periods and necessarily were beginning to lose touch with the cutting-edge developments in their academic disciplines.

The Teachers Institute has four major principles guiding its operation:

> First, teachers of students at different levels can and must interact as colleagues to address the common problems of teaching their disciplines. Second, teacher leadership is crucial in efforts to revitalize public education. Third, teaching is central to the educational process, and teacher-developed materials are essential for student learning. Fourth, the university-school collaboration must be long-term if it is to be truly effective (Vivian 1985b, p. 82).

The institute joins leading scholars from various departments of the university and teachers who have volunteered to become Institute Fellows from the New Haven Public Schools. Working collegially on subjects of interest identified by themselves, the teachers immerse in the process of curriculum design based on the latest scholarship in the field and filtered through the understanding of student needs. Once developed, these curriculum projects are shared with colleagues back in their schools, thus providing additional

*Yale-New Haven Teachers Institute, Box 3563, Yale Station, New Haven, CT 06520-3563; (203) 436-3316.

practical outlets for the work and simultaneously giving the Institute Fellows an opportunity to provide leadership in their own settings. Because the relationship between the university and the public schools is one of long-term duration and because scholarship continues to evolve, teachers are encouraged to participate in the process as many times as it remains useful to each (Vivian 1985b, pp. 83-85).

The program has been evaluated continuously and rigorously by a combination of methods including outside consultants, participant evaluations, surveys of curriculum use, and systemwide quantifiable questionnaires. By all indications, the program is highly successful. Vivian reports that teachers claim improved morale and increased expectations for student performance which, in turn, precipitates improved student performance (Vivian 1985b, p. 86).

Vivian reports that teachers claim improved morale and increased expectations for student performance. . . .

In addition to reporting its overall success, Ascher cautions that the program appears to have no focus on "developing new and effective pedagogy," despite its location in a city in which live large percentages of black or Hispanic students whose families also receive public assistance (1988, p. 20).

The program has been funded from a variety of sources including the university, the New Haven Public Schools, the National Endowment for the Humanities, and other foundations and corporations. In order to solidify the collaboration, Yale has embarked upon a program of fundraising; the goal is to create a $4 million endowment to support the institute.

The Stockton Connection
The Stockton Connection,* begun in 1981, is a partnership between Stockton (N.J.) State College and several central New Jersey school districts. It is included here as much for its program design and outcomes as for its refreshingly honest, self-analytical approach. The program began when several Stockton State faculty members concluded that the college's innovative interdisciplinary general-education approach to liberal arts education and the college's basic skills approach centering on the development of higher-order thinking skills might be used appropriately with precollege students. Accordingly, after finding "some modicum of success" in one school district, the college convinced that district as well as another

*The Stockton Connection, Stockton State College, Jimmy Leeds Rd., Pomona, NJ 08240; (609) 652-1776.

to transfer their staff-development days over to the college (Daly and Jassel 1985, pp. 92-93).

Teacher feedback indicated the results were less spectacular than was hoped. Specifically, teachers cited several factors for their dissatisfaction with the year's inservice effort. They said they believe teacher participation should be voluntary, not mandated; they wanted a greater emphasis on course content rather than on instructional methodologies; they said scattered half days of training were not intensive enough to accomplish the stated goals; and they showed little interest in the purely academic questions raised by Stockton State faculty (Daly and Jassel 1985, pp. 93-94).

In response to these concerns, staff development efforts were changed significantly. The current model offers volunteers an intensive summer seminar week led by Stockton State faculty, with the major focus on recent academic developments in a variety of curriculum areas. Teachers then spend a month in self-guided independent study and curriculum development, seeking ways to incorporate this progress into their instructional plans. The culminating summer event is a second week-long intensive seminar during which the materials are shared, reviewed, and revised. Once the school year begins, teachers test the materials, consult with college faculty, make additional revisions, and share the final results with colleagues from around the state during an annual March conference organized by Stockton State (Wilbur, Lambert, and Young 1987, p. 68).

Teacher participation in both the seminars and the annual conference have increased steadily each year. Evaluations indicate that seminar participants believe the program is highly effective and demanding (Daly and Jassel 1985, pp. 96-97).

OTHER PARTNERSHIP AREAS

Partnerships between high schools and colleges can and do
take many forms. In addition to those already highlighted in
previous sections, several other forms are outlined below.
Some are very old, others still very much are in formation.
No recitation of partnership models ever can be complete,
however. Because partnerships can evolve at any time based
on local needs and because they are limited only by the
breadth of vision of local leadership, the state of the high
school-college partnership is never static.

Preservice Teacher Education Partnerships
Perhaps the oldest area of partnership between schools and
colleges, preservice training of would-be teachers has evolved
around the recognition that preparing teachers should include, at the very least, an opportunity for student teachers
to observe the practice by inservice professionals. In many
cases, of course, college students become involved in activities in addition to observation alone, including tutoring,
working with small groups, and whole-class practice teaching.
Preservice teacher education partnerships would appear to
require a high degree of cooperation between schools and
colleges, but historically such cooperation often has been
lacking. For example, the Holmes Group, a consortium of
94 universities involved in teacher education which has
recommended creating "professional-development schools"
for preservice teacher training, has stated that in order for
these centers to be successful, teachers will have to set aside
their traditional skepticism about the value of assistance from
the ivory tower (Olson 1988, p. 5).

More recently, John Goodlad has characterized the placement of student teachers in schools as haphazard—based
more on convenience than design (Olson 1990, p. 12). He
also has identified "serious disjunctures . . . between the
campus-based portion and the school-based portion" of
teacher education programs (Goodlad May 1990, p. 701).

In addition to the Holmes Group's proposal for professional-development schools, Goodlad's extension of the
concept in what he calls Centers of Pedagogy (Goodlad 1990)
and Irvin's suggestion of a return to a modern-day collaborative adaptation of the single-purpose normal school (1990,
pp. 622-624), others around the country have sought to create
closer ties between universities and schools. One exemplary
model originates at Cleveland State University.

Cleveland State University's Teacher Training Centers

The four main goals of the Teacher Training Centers* are to develop 1) congruence between university instruction and classroom practice; 2) communication between school and university, including shared decision making; 3) a corps of committed classroom teachers who view participation in field experiences as an opportunity for growth; and 4) effective supervision of students' field experiences (Wilbur, Lambert, and Young 1987, p. 60).

Preservice college students are placed in six teacher training centers in urban and suburban settings. The heavy involvement of teacher practitioners in the governance of the centers, as well as through their roles as Classroom Teacher Educators (CTEs), makes this program different from many others. The CTEs are specially trained through graduate courses in the supervision of student teachers. They serve as cooperating teachers, mentors, and resources to the student teachers who work with them and frequently are invited to teach at the university as well. Unlike most models of student teacher placement in which a university representative has authority over a student teacher, the CTEs exercise complete line authority over their college students (Wilbur, Lambert, and Young 1987, pp. 60-61).

Mentoring/Tutoring

It sometimes is difficult to distinguish between tutoring and mentoring programs. The former typically espouse a primary goal of assisting tutees in achieving greater competency in a subject area or more often a skill area such as reading. The latter often aspire to provide mentees with caring, successful, positive role models with whom they can identify and emulate. In practice, programs often attempt to combine elements of both approaches.

Because colleges and universities often can provide a source of educated, skilled, motivated, and committed students, it seems logical that these institutions often participate with high schools in mentoring/tutoring programs. This is especially true in designs aimed at minority, inner-city, at-risk high school students for whom an abundance of positive role models too often is unavailable.

*Teacher Training Centers/Classroom Teacher Educators Program, Rhodes Tower #1348, Cleveland, OH 44115; (216) 687-4616.

Mentoring and mentoring/tutoring models should be examined carefully, however, with respect to outcomes. While these programs would appear to have a certain intuitive validity, data that supports actual changes in mentee or tutee behavior and, specifically, academic performance, too often are lacking. Those who promote and administer these programs would do themselves and others a great service by better documenting the outcomes of their efforts.

One partnership, which has been jointly established by the City University of New York and the New York City Board of Education, is highlighted here.

City University of New York (CUNY) and New York City Board of Education's Student Mentoring Project

The partnership of this project* began in 1985 with funding provided by the New York State legislature to expand the relationship between three CUNY colleges and four local high schools (Tyler, Gruber, and McMullan 1987, p. 97). The project has grown to include 20 public high schools and 14 CUNY colleges.

The project's goals are to provide tutoring and mentoring to increase retention rates of high school students with academic difficulties; to provide college students as positive peer models; to provide opportunities for public service to college students while introducing them to teaching careers; and to recruit students for the colleges (Tyler, Gruber, and McMullan 1987, pp. 97–98).

The college students are volunteers, but they may receive course credit for their work. In addition, they are trained to be effective tutors and mentors (City University of New York 1985). A mentor handbook has been developed for use in conjunction with the mentor training experience (Kwalick et al 1988).

Students who are served by the mentors show many signs of being potential dropouts: 66.1 percent are poor; absenteeism is high, with each mentee averaging 12 days of absences prior to program involvement; and 40 percent of ninth graders and 55 percent of tenth graders show reading scores registering at the elementary school level. Most mentees are 16 years old or younger (Tyler, Gruber, and McMullan 1987, pp. v, viii).

*Student Mentoring Project, City University of New York, 351 West 18th St., Room 236, New York, NY 10011; (212) 645-4141.

Mentors themselves range in age from 18 to their late 50s. In some cases, the ethnicity of the mentees and mentors parallel each other; in other cases, marked differences exist. Seventy-five percent of mentors are women, 50 percent are black, and 25 percent are Hispanic (Tyler, Gruber, and McMullan 1987, pp. 101-102).

In addition to cooperating at the CUNY-Board of Education institutional planning level, site coordinators at the colleges and high schools are encouraged to display initiative in administrating and designing the program at each location. Thus, programs vary greatly from site to site.

Many observers and participants agree that the program can be improved. The issue of the role of tutoring in skills areas as part of the mentoring process is of particular concern. In many cases, programs have emphasized interpersonal relations and personal decision making at the expense, some say, of remedial work. On the positive side, the more than 200 mentees report receiving significant help from mentors in working out their personal problems and 60 percent of mentees report that mentors helped them in setting personal goals. Nearly 90 percent of the high school students say they would recommend the program to a friend; 80 percent say they would join the program again if given the opportunity (Tyler, Gruber, and McMullan 1987, pp. 116-120).

The CUNY/Board of Education Student Mentoring Project shows an obvious, if not wholly intentional, overlap between mentoring and tutoring. However, the Kenmore Project, described next, displays a greater unity of purpose.

The Kenmore High School/University of Akron Kenmore Project

The Kenmore Project,* initiated in 1984, is a partnership with a clear focus: It is a high school and a university collaborating to support the high school's writing program by utilizing college-student volunteers.

College students involved in the project all are enrolled in an English instructional methodology course which meets at least one session a week at the high school. In addition to the standard course work and lectures, students observe high school English classes, tutor high school students in writ-

*The Kenmore Project, University of Akron, Akron, OH 44325; (216) 375-6971.

ing, grade papers, meet with teachers, and lead discussion groups. Students also are assigned to observe a regular English class for a semester. Through this class, they observe the teacher on a continuing basis, meet with students one to one, and participate in course planning.

College students also can volunteer to work alongside regular teachers in the high school's writing lab in which the students can opt for additional nonremedial assistance in their writing development.

For the college students, the Kenmore Project provides an opportunity to really understand what teaching English is all about. Also, it provides a laboratory for the students in which they can compare and contrast what they are learning in their college methodology class with the realities they see before them each day in the high school English classroom. The high school and its students, on the other hand, reap the benefits of 20 or more eager helpers to support its writing program.

The Kenmore Project in 1985 was declared a "Center of Excellence" by the National Conference of Teachers of English (Wilbur, Lambert, and Young 1987, p. 89).

Partnerships for School Improvement or Restructuring

Several examples reflect partnerships whose principal goal is to improve or restructure an existing school or set of schools. In some cases, the partnerships operate at a statewide level; in others, the focus might be a city or suburban school system or a sub-set of those schools. In fewer cases, the movement is national in scope.

Local reform partnerships

The Boston Compact. The Boston Compact,* unlike most of the other partnerships discussed previously, began as a joint project of a troubled public school system and business leaders (Gross 1988, p. 4). The compact was formed in 1982, when Boston was still reeling from its attempts at responding to court-ordered desegregation. The terms of the compact, signed Sept. 22, 1982, called for the public schools to improve attendance, reduce the dropout rate, and improve skills achievement. In exchange, the business community agreed to hire more high school graduates and provide summer

*The Boston Compact, 110 Tremont St., Boston, MA 02125; (617) 726-6200.

employment opportunities to high school students who were still in school.

In November 1983, the compact added an agreement with a group which represented the Boston area's major colleges and universities, committing these schools to increased enrollment targets for the graduates of Boston's high schools. In 1984, 27 trade unions also joined the compact, pledging positions in apprenticeships.

Although the role initially delineated for the colleges and universities merely was to accept more high school graduates from the Boston schools, their participation actually grew to include project participation in several compact activities, including "Compact Ventures." This initiative was aimed at high-risk ninth graders and involved, among many other aspects, college-student volunteers who provided tutoring and mentoring.

Evaluation of the program has revealed that between 1982 and 1985, attendance improved along with academic achievement. While a few exceptions are noted, the dropout rates of most schools have remained high at 16 percent, despite interventions. Job placement goals have been met or surpassed.

Funding for the Boston Compact came from a variety of sources including the Massachusetts Office of Economic Affairs, and local businesses, universities, and labor unions provided funds and contributed work (Orr 1987, pp. 177-188).

Other partnerships have sought to bring school systems and universities together to create unprecedented governance systems. One such example is the relationship between Boston University and the Chelsea, Mass., public schools, through which the university administers the schools under a management contract. A second far-reaching effort is the alliance between a Colorado school district and the University of Southern Colorado, described here.

University of Southern Colorado/School District 60 Alliance. In a plan* that began operation in July 1991, Edmund Villejo, the superintendent of the 18,000-student Colorado School District 60 in Pueblo, became a vice president of the 4,300-student University of Southern Colorado. As vice

*University of Southern Colorado/School District 60 Alliance, University of Southern Colorado, 2200 Bonforte Blvd., Pueblo, CO 81001; (719) 549-2306.

president, he reports both to the university's president, Robert Shirley, and to the school district's board of education.

The goals of this rather unusual venture are to develop closer curricular coordination between the institutions, as well as to seek creative ways to use college and public school teachers. In addition, the university president is expected to play a significant role along with the superintendent and the board of education in goal setting, budgeting, strategic planning, and developing "a system for rewarding or penalizing schools based on their performance" (Bradley 1990, p. 5).

It is hoped that these actions will result in improved academic performance—especially for the district's Hispanic population—in the Pueblo school district. The university, which is administered under that state's department of agriculture, expects to benefit in that its education majors are permitted to use the public schools for intensive preservice experiences. While the education students will receive the most immediate benefit, it is expected that other departments at the university also will play significant roles in the project.

Other benefits that might be realized by the university are increased student recruitment from the school district and better skills preparation for incoming students, leading to lowered costs for remedial services upon admission to the university.

Colorado's governor, legislators, and officials of the state education department have expressed support for the alliance. Their cooperation will be necessary to secure waivers from regulations. For example, if university faculty teach in the public schools without traditional public school certification, a waiver will be required. Another possible area of exception would be created if, upon the retirement of the superintendent, the school board decided to hire a university administrator or a business person as superintendent rather than a more traditionally qualified candidate.

Statewide reform partnerships

Many examples of statewide reform efforts involving schools and universities could be cited. Two ongoing efforts are those of California's Achievement Council and Mississippi's Project '95.

California's Achievement Council. The Achievement Council, Inc.,* is noted for its clarion call for the integration of public and private resources in order to better serve the predominantly Hispanic, black, and low-income student population of its public schools. In a series of reports, the council suggests strategies to address the gaps in the education of the state's minority and poor students (Haycock and Navarro 1988). It advocates public and private ventures, university-school partnerships, and local and regional systematic planning, among other techniques; the focus typically is on student academic achievement in school (Haycock and Brown 1984).

The council's recommendations have been adopted in many locales throughout the state, including the Los Angeles Unified School District, which had experienced a 43 percent attrition rate in its schools. The district's Dropout Prevention and Recovery program (DPR), which was piloted in 1985-86 in 24 elementary, junior high, and high schools, incorporated many of the Achievement Council proposals (Los Angeles Unified School District 1986).

Mississippi's Project '95. Begun in spring 1990, Project '95† represents an attempt to get Mississippi's three major public education governing bodies—the Board of Trustees of State Institutions of Higher Learning, the State Board for Community and Junior Colleges, and the State Board of Education—to work more cohesively to raise standards throughout the state at all levels of education. Specifically, the state was concerned with the fragmented, loosely governed nature of its educational system, in which each constituency had its own mission and educational philosophy (Southerland, Leonard, Edwards, and Hutto 1990, p. 1). The current lack of articulation is not, of course, unique to Mississippi; what is unique is the state's apparent willingness to address it in such a forthright manner.

Project '95's three major goals are 1) to bridge the academic gap between high school and college and to accentuate teacher training and retraining with special emphasis on high schools; 2) to make college and university programs more accessible and attractive to minority students; and 3) to strengthen college and university admissions requirements

*The Achievement Council, Inc., 1016 Castro St., Oakland, CA 94607.

†Project '95, Institutions of Higher Learning, 3825 Ridgewood Rd., Jackson, MS 39211-6453; (601) 982-6457.

by the year 1995, placing a new emphasis on academic content (Board of Trustees of State Institutions of Higher Learning, State Board for Community and Junior Colleges, and State Board of Education 1990).

In order to achieve these goals, a variety of special projects have been planned, including collaborative mini-grants, regional financial and publicity campaigns, regional financial aid workshops, Title II summer institutes, and participation in the College Board's Educational EQuality (EQ) Project. Project leaders also have prepared a draft of new, strengthened admissions requirements for community colleges and universities.

. . . What is unique is the state's apparent willingness to address [its poor articulation] in such a forthright manner.

Nationwide reform partnerships

Several nationwide efforts at school-college partnerships have been organized. One is the National Network for Educational Renewal, aimed chiefly at affecting state policy makers (Goodlad 1988). A second is the Coalition of Essential Schools, led by Theodore Sizer, which began as a partnership between Brown University and schools in Rhode Island and Massachusetts and which more recently has grown to include local affiliates throughout the nation (Sizer). Member schools must agree to adhere to the principles that have grown out of Sizer's research into school improvement, developed at Brown (Ascher 1988, p. 26; Sizer 1984).

Another significant effort is the Council of Chief State School Officers' School/College Collaboration Project. Begun in 1983 and funded continuously since then by the Mellon Foundation, the project has shifted its focus several times since inception. Starting with a thrust toward encouraging college-school collaborative projects through a program of local mini-grants, the emphasis then shifted to projects aimed at teacher education. The latest concentration has been on improving teaching for at-risk populations in inner cities and isolated rural areas (Council of Chief State School Officers 1988; Ascher 1988, p. 28).

Of all the national projects, however, perhaps none has been so sweeping or as well known as the EQ Models Program for School-College Collaboration of the College Board's Educational EQuality (EQ) Project, described next.

EQ Models Program for School-College Collaboration.
The EQ Models Program for School-College Collaboration*
is an important component of the College Board's Educational
EQuality (EQ) Project, launched in 1980. The project's long-
term goals are to improve the quality of secondary education
and to ensure equal access to postsecondary education for
all students (College Board Annual Report 1989, p. 23).
Among its major outcomes are the publication of six books
highlighting recommendations for the college-preparatory
high school curriculum (College Board 1983). The Educational EQuality Project also has commissioned research into
quality teaching and learning, among other subjects, and
sponsored colloquia on allied topics.

The EQ Models Program for School-College Collaboration
began in May of 1987 with a conference which included representatives of 18 pairs of schools and colleges. This network
has grown to embrace 125 school systems or individual high
schools and 60 colleges and universities (College Board
1987).

The models, while otherwise differing widely, have five
common characteristics: school-college partnerships, at-risk
students, improved academic preparation of students through
curricular and instructional emphases, use of high school and
college expertise and other community resources to improve
student academic achievement, and discussion of experiences
and results with others (Wilbur, Lambert, and Young 1987,
p. 77).

The schools and colleges in the program represent both
public and private institutions; regional, racial, ethnic, and
financial diversity; and a blend of urban, suburban, and rural
areas. Ascher reports that "the activities of the individual partnerships comprise student outreach and support . . . teacher
professional development, curriculum improvement, parent
and community outreach, and research" (1988, p. 27). She
also cites several case studies that have been sponsored by
the project, including Adelman 1988, Sosniak 1988, and Van
De Water 1988.

---

*EQ Models Program for School-College Collaboration, Office of Academic
Affairs, The College Board, 45 Columbus Ave., New York, NY 10023-6917;
(212) 858-2800.

CONCLUSION

Summary and Review

It is clear an increased awareness of high school-college partnerships exists, especially in the higher education community. This is evident in the increased numbers of partnerships, legislative activity, publications, news reports, foundation and agency support, and conferences and panels devoted to the subject.

While the roots of the (often strained) relationships between high schools and colleges go back two centuries or more, the closer collaboration successful partnerships require is a relatively recent phenomenon.

Many reasons explain this burgeoning interest, including a changing student population, a more democratic higher education admissions policy, students' frequent lack of skills preparedness, an increasing awareness for the need for new models of inservice staff development for high school teachers, and greater competition in college-student recruitment. Additionally, awareness of the need for enhanced articulation between levels of institutions by administrators, parents, and state education department officials has increased, as has the awareness that the challenges confronting contemporary secondary education—especially at-risk students, women, and minorities—require a community of effort in which colleges have been asked to play a much larger role than previously reserved for them.

As a result of these and other factors, a variety of partnership forms have developed. Examples include concurrent-enrollment programs such as the College Board's Advanced Placement Program and Syracuse University's Project Advance, both for well-above-average students; LaGuardia Community College's Middle College High School and Florida International's Partners in Progress Program, for students at risk; and Minnesota's Postsecondary Enrollment Options Program, for students of all ability levels, are just a few examples of such programs.

Other partnerships focus on enrichment, compensatory, and motivational concerns. These models are typified by programs such as the University of California's MESA program, Colorado Community College's Partners program, the Center for the Advancement of Academically Talented Youth at Johns Hopkins University, and the University of St. Louis Partnership for Progress Bridge Program.

Many partnerships have taken the form of academic alliances and other kinds of teacher-to-teacher partnerships. Examples are the Greater Boston Foreign Language Collaborative, an excellent example of the academic alliance movement; the National Writing Project; the Atlanta Public Schools Project with the National Faculty; and the Yale-New Haven Teachers Institute.

Other partnerships have developed in the areas of pre-service teacher education (such as Cleveland State University's teacher training centers), mentoring/tutoring programs (the University of Akron's Kenmore Project, for example), and partnerships which have as their objective school improvement or restructuring (such as Mississippi's Project '95 and the College Board's EQ Models Program for School-College Collaboration).

The movement toward partnerships has not been without its inherent impediments, however. Chief among these have been the long-recognized cultural discontinuities between high schools and colleges that have sprung from differences in institutional funding and resources, the student bodies, teachers and teaching (including teaching load, student characteristics, source and availability of materials of instruction, academic freedom, salaries and vacations, teaching amenities, teaching qualifications, valuing performance, and rewards), faculty roles in decision making, and institutional leadership style. Each of these factors—at one time or another, when not adequately considered—has led to mistrust, institutional and/or individual jealousy, an inability to produce a common agenda, and failure.

Recommendations for Future Practice

In spite of these impediments, interest in establishing partnerships is increasing. What issues and actions should an institution consider when contemplating involvement in partnerships with high schools?

• *Identify the student population and program goals.* Since many different partnership models are possible and each has its own strengths and limitations, the most important decisions are identifying the student body and the program goals. Once this information is identified, other decisions will fall into place.

In some respects, these initial decisions might define the nature and level of community support the program will receive, and this might affect institutional decision making.

Some institutions have solved this dilemma by setting up several programs—each with its own special target group.

• *Contact local high schools and school districts.* With the exception of a few national efforts, most partnerships are local or regional in nature. In any case, often the best way to initiate a successful program is to start locally within the secondary and postsecondary school community of interest.

Another advantage of a local liaison is that lines of communication, if only between people from a college admissions-services staff and high school college counseling personnel, probably already exist. Networking can be very important in setting up a new collaborative venture; it always is easier to build on relationships than to rely on building new ones.

It is crucial to consider why high schools might want to become involved in dual-enrollment plans. It is imperative that higher education leaders know these reasons and understand the natural distrust with which high school personnel often regard the motives of colleges seeking linkages. Therefore, any consideration of institution-to-institution partnerships must begin by considering the commitment of institutional leadership. This particularly is true in the case of high school-college partnerships. College presidents and high school principals must manifest their bilateral interest in the collaborative process if success is to be regarded as a realistic possibility.

Since the mission and the student body of a community or junior college, a major research university, a highly selective liberal arts college, or a selective engineering school differ so markedly, choosing an appropriate high school and target population within a high school also can be very important in meeting program objectives.

Of course, some high schools previously have established partnerships with colleges. Others might be willing to do so, especially if the advantages to the high school are evident. A good place to initiate a dialogue is with either the superintendent of schools or the high school principal.

• *Determine costs.* Costs are associated with the start-up of every new program; costs are associated with sustaining the program, as well. No hard and fast rules exist to say which program model is the most cost efficient—each is a special blend of costs and benefits. A realistic approach is to evaluate the likely costs based on the implementation of the model or models identified.

Among those to consider are the following: program administration, local and regional travel, printing recruitment materials, student testing, counseling, application fees, transcript fees, student tuition, scholarships based on need and/or ability, staff development, curriculum development, instructional materials and supplies, college text books, smaller-than-average class size, teacher personnel costs, student evaluation, space, and program evaluation.

Sources of support also should be considered, including the school district, students and parents, the college, the state education department, legislative grants and laws, foundations, and endowments.

Political, economic, and legal considerations also affect the analysis. For example, some states might not permit students in public school settings to pay tuition for a college class taken as part of their regular high school instructional day. In other states, this practice might be permitted as long as participation is voluntary. In still other localities, the practice might be acceptable as long as financial aid is available to students from low-income families. A few states solve the problem by paying the tuition for all students from state funds— either channeling payments directly to students or, more likely, to cooperating colleges or local school districts.

• *Develop community support.* Even after investigating all the factors discussed previously, a college still must face the challenge of selling its community on the merits of the program model(s) selected.

Building support for the program in the high school community is a second consideration. Parents might be solicited through direct-mail efforts by the high school or the college, or both. News releases to community newspapers often are used to raise community consciousness about a program. Another effective medium is a meeting for parents in which the program's benefits are explained.

All such efforts should stress those elements which will appeal to parents in the community while honestly representing what involvement means and does not mean. Program costs to be borne by parents must be clearly described.

It is vital that tentative or unsupportable claims aren't made. Two examples: In a new concurrent-enrollment program, it typically is unclear how credits earned through the program will transfer to other colleges. This must be made clear. Although it generally is true that a precollegiate record of college-level accomplishment will help with admission to more selective colleges, this cannot be guaranteed.

• *Evaluate for Program Improvement.* Often in the enthusiasm to start a new program, a most critical element in long-range success is overlooked: program evaluation. Program evaluation ought to be considered early in the life of a partnership program. For one, both colleges and school districts will want to see evidence that their investment of resources is justified. And, in order for a program director to improve a program, it is necessary to implement some means of evaluating that program.

Evaluation can and should include many factors, populations, and techniques. Factors to examine, depending upon program goals, might include the following: academic achievement, degree of satisfaction with program elements, transferability of credit, attendance, costs, quality of instruction, number and demography of students participating, number of college credits and classes registered for through programs, college application rate of program participants, postsecondary program-participant performance, and participant satisfaction.

A variety of techniques may be used to conduct program evaluation. Standardized tests, pretests and posttests, surveys, questionnaires, statistical data analysis, and interviews with program participants are among the most common evaluation techniques.

While the natural tendency is to evaluate the effect of program intervention on participants, other significant constituencies also may be taken into account. High school and college teachers and administrators, parents, school board members, college admissions officers, and community-opinion leaders should be included as valuable data sources.

Many times, the most successful evaluation design consists of a consortium approach through which many interested parties combine their efforts and perspectives to more thoroughly evaluate the program than each party alone might have been able to achieve.

Recommendations for Future Research
Because the field of high school-college partnerships still is actively developing, significant research issues remain to be

addressed. These issues tend to fall into three major areas: descriptive, analysis of process, and analysis of outcomes.

Descriptive research

The field of high school-college partnerships is both youthful and dynamic. As a result, most knowledge about the extent of these partnership practices is either secondhand or an often informal estimate. Even major efforts at counting, describing, and categorizing the phenomena rely heavily on self-reporting rather than on the expertise of outside researchers. It doesn't help that partnerships fall on both sides of the great divide between high schools and colleges—thereby theoretically representing interest to both secondary- and postsecondary-education researchers. In actuality, however, the topics are the province of neither.

In addition to ambitious efforts already under way, we need, then, a more comprehensive national census of high school-college partnerships—one that can assure that all extant models and programs will be counted and cataloged.

We need to know a great deal more about the demography of these efforts. What kinds of institutions initiate them? How are they funded? What are the characteristics—gender, ethnicity, age, achievement, experience, income, educational attainment, and skills—of program participants? When were programs founded? What are the characteristics of the services?

Analysis of process

Along with the need to more comprehensively catalog high school-college partnerships, we have a concomitant need to gain greater insight into the process of their creation, operation, and, if it should occur, their demise. Only now is a body of research beginning to emerge which attempts to document the process by which colleges and high schools work together. The distinction between cooperation and collaboration, for example, is one outcome.

We must understand the effects of cultural discontinuity, which seems constantly to pull at the fabric of a partnership even as its cooperants would attempt to weave it. Sociologists or cultural anthropologists might have much to discuss about this topic.

Another possible research area is the initiation process of partnerships. How are they initiated, by whom, and for what reasons? What local, regional, or national dynamics set these initiatives into motion? What are the roles played by educational reformers, national associations, agencies and foundations in promoting this process? Would a lack of interest by these entities reflect a possible waning of interest at the institutional level or, perhaps, precipitate it?

When operational, how do these programs function? What are their governance structures? What is the interplay between policy making and administrative practice? Are the programs, even if one assumes they collaboratively have been planned, collaboratively operated? Need they be?

When partnership programs are discontinued, what are the reasons? Who is involved in making the decision to pull the plug? These and many other questions of process need to be investigated by serious researchers. Too much of what we know today about the process is the result of interested self-reporting. We need additional, less subjective observers to help provide a more complete picture.

Analysis of outcomes

Again, as might be expected because of the relatively short period of time many high school-partnerships have existed, research into the outcomes of many partnerships has been limited. Advanced Placement, Project Advance, College Now, Middle College, the National Writing Project, Johns Hopkins' CTY, the Yale-New Haven Teachers Institute, and others have generated a large body of outcome-based data. But these truly are exceptions.

Most "model" programs, indeed, receive this appellation because of reputational reports, because they are sponsored and supported by prominent organizations, or because they fill a certain definitional or categorical niche. None of these explanations undermines the probable outstanding worth of such programs; at the same time, these accolades tend all too often to obscure the need for outcome analysis.

We need more complete data on what happens to program participants before, during, and after their involvement with a partnership. Do teachers in any particular teacher-to-teacher partnership feel better about themselves during participation? If so, how long does this effect last? If not, why? Does program satisfaction ultimately translate into changed teaching practices? Do their students consequently perform better, exhibit greater insight, change their levels of conceptualization, or master the subject content or skills better?

We need to gain insight, as well, into the long- and short-term effects, if any, of these programs on their sponsoring institutions, on surrounding communities, and on other program participants and contributors. What are the implications for staff development, curriculum, institutional planning, school reform and restructuring, student and teacher recruitment, interinstitutional governance, and local, state, regional, and national social and education policy?

Unless a sound sense of the realistic anticipated outcomes of high school-college partnerships can be established, their future viability cannot be assured; nor, perhaps, can they even appropriately be justified apart from the accounts of their many and still increasing supporters.

REFERENCES

The Educational Resources Information Center (ERIC) Clearinghouse on Higher Education abstracts and indexes the current literature on higher education for inclusion in ERIC's data base and announcement in ERIC's monthly bibliographic journal, *Resources in Education* (RIE). Most of these publications are available through the ERIC Document Reproduction Service (EDRS). For publications cited in this bibliography that are available from EDRS, ordering number and price code are included. Readers who wish to order a publication should write to the ERIC Document Reproduction Service, 7420 Fullerton Rd., Suite 110, Springfield, VA 22153-2852. (Phone orders with VISA or MasterCard are taken at 800-443-ERIC or 703-440-1400.) When ordering, please specify the document (ED) number. Documents are available as noted in microfiche (MF) and paper copy (PC). If you have the price code ready when you call EDRS, an exact price can be quoted. The last page of the latest issue of *Resources in Education* also has the current cost, listed by code.

Adelman, N. 1988. "Collaborative Professional Development: A Report on Structures, Facilitation, and Outcomes of Collaborative Teacher Professional Development in the Educational EQuality Project's Models Program for School-College Collaboration." Draft. New York: The College Board.

Albert, L. March 1990. "In This Issue." *AAHE Bulletin: 2*

Ascher, C. 1988. *School-College Collaborations: A Strategy for Helping Low-Income Minorities.* New York: ERIC Clearinghouse on Urban Education and Institute for Urban and Minority Education. ED 306 339. 30 pp. MF–01; PC–02.

———. 1958. "A look at Continuity in School Programs." Washington, D.C.: Association for Supervision and Curriculum Development, National Education Association.

"Average Faculty Salaries, 1989-90." Sept. 5, 1990. *Chronicle of Higher Education:* 23.

Bagasao, P.Y. March 1990. "An Update From AAHE's National Project in Support of Academic Alliances." *AAHE Bulletin:* 6.

Beckhard, R. 1975. "Organization Development in Large Systems." In *The Laboratory Method of Changing and Learing,* edited by K.D. Benne, L.P. Bradford, J.R. Gibb, and R.O. Lippet. Palo Alto, Ca.: Science and Behavior Books.

Bender, T. Winter 1986. "The University and the Egalitarian Ideal." *New York University Magazine.*

Berman, P. November 1985. "The Next Step: The Minnesota Plan." *Phi Delta Kappan:* 188–193.

Blanchard, B.E. 1971. *A National Survey of Curriculum Articulation Between the College of Liberal Arts and the Secondary School.* Chicago: De Paul University.

———. 1975. *A New System of Education.* Homewood, Ill.: E.T.C. Publications.

Boyer, E.L. 1983. *High School: A Report on Secondary Education in America*. New York: Harper and Row.

———. April 1984. "Reflections on the Great Debate of '83." *Phi Delta Kappan*: 525–530.

———. 1987. *College: The Undergraduate Experience in America*. New York: Harper and Row.

Board of Trustees of State Institutions of Higher Learning, State Board for Community and Junior Colleges, and State Board of Education. 1990. *Project '95*. Jackson, Miss.

Bradley, A. October 24, 1990. "Colorado District, University to Form Unusual Alliance." *Education Week*.

Brizius, M., and H. Cooper. 1984. *A Joining of Hands: State Policies and Programs to Improve High School-College Linkages*. Alexandria, Va.: National Association of State Boards of Education.

Broatch, L. Fall 1989. "Keeping Minds in Motion: The Schooling of Minority Engineers." *College Board Review*: 40–45+. EJ399338.

Byrd, C.W., Jr. "Academic Alliances: School/College Faculty Collaboratives." *Foreign Language Annals, 18(1)*.

California State Postsecondary School Education Commission. January 1989. *The Effectiveness of the Mathematics, Engineering, Science Achievement (MESA) Program's Administrative and Policy-Making Processes*. A report to the legislature in response to assembly bill 610 (1985). Commission Report No. 89-4. ED 307 131. MF-01; PC-02.

Carnegie Commission on Higher Education. 1971. *Less Time, More Options: Education Beyond the High School*. New York: McGraw-Hill.

———. 1973. *Continuity and Discontinuity: Higher Education and the Schools*. New York: McGraw-Hill.

Carnegie Council on Policy Studies in Higher Education. 1979. *Giving Youth a Better Chance: Options for Education, Work and Service*. San Francisco: Jossey-Bass.

Carnegie Forum on Education and the Economy. 1986. *A Nation Prepared: Teachers for the 21st Century—The Report of the Task Force on Teaching as a Profession*. New York: Author.

Casserly, P.L. 1965. *Colleges' Decisions on Advanced Placement: A Follow-Up of Advanced Placement Candidates of 1963*. Princeton, N.J.: Educational Testing Service.

Chira, S. March 24, 1991. "The Big Test: How to Translate the Talk About School Reform Into Action." *The New York Times*, section 4, pp. 1, 4.4

City University of New York. June 1985. *Collaborative Programs: Schools and Colleges Working Together*. New York: Author.

Cohen, A.M., and F.B. Brawer. 1989. *The American Community College* (2nd ed.). San Francisco: Jossey-Bass.

The College Board. 1983. *Academic Preparation for College: What Students Need to Know and Be Able to Do*. New York: Author.

———. 1987. *EQ Models Program for School–College Collaboration.*
New York: Author.

———. 1989. *The College Board Annual Report: 1987-88.* New York:
Author.

Commission on the Humanities. 1980. *The Humanities in American
Life.* Berkeley: The University of California Press.

Council of Chief State School Officers. 1988. *School/College Collaboration: Fact Sheet.* Washington, D.C.: Author.

Cullen, C., and M.G. Moed. 1988. "Serving High Risk Adolescents."
In *Collaborating with High Schools,* edited by Janet E. Lieberman,
37–49. New Directions for Community Colleges No. 63. San Francisco: Jossey-Bass.

Daly, W.T., and L. Jassel. 1985. "Continuous Content Updating: The
Stockton Connection." In *College-School Collaboration: Appraising
the Major Approaches,* edited by William T. Daly, 79–89. New Directions for Teaching and Learning No. 24. San Francisco: Jossey-Bass.

Durden, W.G. 1985. "Early Instruction by the College: Johns Hop-
kins's Center for Talented Youth." *In College-School Collaboration:
Appraising the Major Approaches,* edited by W.T. Daly, 37–46. New
Directions for Teaching and Learning No. 24. San Francisco: Jossey-
Bass.

Eurich, A.C., and J.J. Scanton. 1960. "Articulation in Educational
Units." In C.W. Harris (ed.), *Encyclopedia of Educational Research.*
New York: Macmillan.

"Florida Administrative Code, Rule 6A-10.241." 1983. Author.

Frost, J.A. 1972. "Time-Shortening and Articulation." In W.L. Godwin
and P.B. Mann (eds.), *Higher Education: Myths, Realities and Possibilities.* Atlanta: South Regional Education Board.

Fund for the Advancement of Education. 1953. *Bridging the Gap
Between School and College.* New York: Author.

———. 1957. *They Went to College Early.* New York: Author.

Garms, W.I., J.W. Guthrie and L.C. Pierce. 1978. *School Finance: The
Economics and Politics of Public Education.* Englewood Cliffs,
N.J.: Prentice-Hall.

Gaudiani, C. 1985. "Local Communities of Inquiry: Penn's Academic
Alliances Program." In *College-School Collaboration: Appraising
the Major Approaches,* edited by W.T. Daly, 69-78. New Directions
for Teaching and Learning No. 24. San Francisco: Jossey-Bass. EJ
330 091.

Gaudiani, C., and D. Burnett. 1986. *Academic Alliances: A New
Approach to School-College Collaboration.* Washington, D.C.: Amer-
ican Association of Higher Education. ED 276 383. MF–01;
PC–02.

Gerhard, D. 1955. "Emergence of the Credit System in American Education Considered as a Problem of Social and Intellectual History."
American Association of University Professors Bulletin 41.

Goodlad, J.I. 1988. "School-University Partnerships for Educational

Renewal: Rationale and Concepts." In *School-University Partnerships in Action: Concepts, Cases & Concerns,* by K.A. Sirotnik and J.I. Goodlad. New York Teachers College Press.

————. May 1990. "Studying the Education of Educators: From Conception to Findings." *Phi Delta Kappan,* 698–701.

————. 1990. *Teachers for Our Nation's Schools.* San Francisco: Jossey-Bass.

Gray, J. 1985. "Joining a National Network: The National Writing Project." In *College-School Collaboration: Appraising the Major Approaches,* edited by W.T. Daly, 61-68. New Directions for Teaching and Learning No. 24. San Francisco: Jossey-Bass.

————. 1986. "University of California, Berkeley: The Bay Area Writing Project and the National Writing Project." In *School-College Collaboration Programs,* edited by R. Fortune. New York: Modern Language Association.

Greenberg, A.R. 1982. "High School/College Articulated Programs: Pooling Resources Across the Abyss. *National Association of Secondary School Principals Bulletin* 66(454).

————. 1987. "College Study in High School for Low and Moderate Achievers." Ed.D. dissertation, Teachers College, Columbia University, New York.

————. 1989. *Concurrent Enrollment Programs: College Credit for High School Students.* Bloomington, In: Phi Delta Kappa Educational Foundation.

Gross, T.L. 1988. *Partners in Education.* San Francisco: Jossey-Bass.

Hanson, H.P. Spring 1980. "Twenty-Five Years of the Advanced Placement Program." *The College Board Review.*

Haycock, K., and P.R. Brown. 1984. *Excellence for Whom?* A Report from the Planning Committee for the Achievement Council. Oakland, Ca.: The Achievement Council, Inc. ED 277 787. MF–01; PC–04.

Haycock, K., and M.S. Navarro. May 1988. *Unfinished Business: Fulfilling Our Children's Promise.* A Report from the Achievement Council. Oakland, Ca.: The Achievement Council, Inc. ED 299 025. MF–01; PC–02.

Hoyt, K. 1978. *A Concept of Collaboration in Career Education.* Washington, D.C.: United States Office of Education.

Irvin, G. April 1990. "Collaborative Teacher Education." *Phi Delta Kappan.*

Kintzer, F.C. 1973. *Middleman in Higher Education: Improving Articulation Among High School, Community College, and Senior Institutions.* San Francisco: Jossey-Bass.

Kwalick, B. et al. "CUNY/BOE Student Mentor Project: A Collaborative Program." Mentor handbook. New York: City University of New York, Office of Urban Affairs; New York City Board of Education. ED 302 759. MF–01; PC–02.

Lambert, L.M. 1985. *A Profile of Syracuse University Project Advance*

Students: SAT Scores and Rank-in-Class Data. Syracuse, NY: Syracuse University, Center for Instructional Development.

Lieberman, J. February 1986. "Ford Foundation Proposal." Long Island City, N.Y.: LaGuardia Community College.

Los Angeles Unified School District. April 1986. Los Angeles Unified School District Dropout Prevention and Recovery (DPR) Program. Los Angeles: Author. ED 274 727. MF–01; PC–02.

Maeroff, G.I. 1983. *School and College: Partnerships in Education.* Princeton: Carnegie Foundation for the Advancement of Teaching.

"Mainstreaming Academic Partnerships." March 1990. *AAHE Bulletin:* 5.

Martin, D.C., D.W. Mocker, and N.C. Brown. 1986. *Joining Forces for Urban Youth.* Washington, D.C.: National Association of State Universities and Land-Grant Colleges.

Menacker, J. 1975. *From School to College: Articulation and Transfer.* Washington, D.C.: American Council on Education.

Miller, J.W. 1968. *Male Student Success in the Collegiate Early Admission Experiment.* Honolulu: University of Hawaii Press. ED O68 017.

"Minnesota 1985 Omnibus School Aids Act," Article 5, Section 1, Subdivision 4. August 2, 1985. Author, 10.

Mocker, D.W., D.C. Martin, and N.C. Brown. April 1988. "Lessons Learned from Collaboration." Urban Education, 23(1), 42–50.

National Commission on Excellence in Education. 1983. *A Nation at Risk: The Imperative for Educational Reform.* Washington, D.C.: United States Department of Education.

The National Faculty: Distinguished Scholars Serving the Nation's Schools. 1987. Atlanta: National Faculty of Humanities, Arts, and Science.

"Number of Students in AP Program Nearly Triples in Past Decade." April 1985. *Phi Delta Kappan.*

Olson, L. February 10, 1988. "Holmes Group Seeks Closer Ties with Schools." *Education Week.*

———. October 24, 1990. "Goodlad Teacher-Education Study Calls for 'Centers of Pedagogy'." *Education Week.*

Orr, M.T. 1987. *Keeping Students in School: A Guide to Effective Dropout Prevention Programs and Strategies.* San Francisco: Jossey-Bass.

Osborn, J.W. 1928. *Overlapping and Omission in Our Course of Study.* Bloomington, Ill.: Public School Publishing Company.

Parnell, D. 1985. *The Neglected Majority.* Washington, D.C.: The Community College Press.

Phillips, R.G. 1987. Partners in Education Black Student Opportunity Program. Miami: Miami-Dade Community College.

"Prefreshman Summer Immersion Program Gives 7,000 CUNY Students an Academic Boost." 1989. *The Freshman Year Experience Newsletter* 2(2).

Pressey, S.L. 1949. *Educational Acceleration: Appraisals and Basic Problems.* Columbus: Ohio State University Press.

Quality Education for Minorities Project. 1990. *Education that Works: An Action Plan for the Education of Minorities.* Cambridge: Massachusetts Institute of Technology.

Ramist, L. 1984. "Predictive Validity of the AP Tests." In T.F. Donlon (ed.), *The College Board Technical Handbook for the Scholastic Aptitude Test and Achievement Tests:* 141–170. New York: College Entrance Examination Board.

Randall, R. May 1986. "Options Are Changing the Face of Education in Minnesota." *The School Administrator.*

Raughton, J. L., et al. 1989. "Mid-Term Report on Partners Program." Washington, D.C.: Paper presented at the Annual Convention of the American Association of Community and Junior Colleges. ED 306 976. MF–01; PC–01.

Rosovsky, H. 1990. *The University: An Owner's Manual.* New York: W.W. Norton.

Rothman, R. October 15, 1986. "Enrollment Gains Linked to Marketing." *Education Week:* 8.

"School-College Partnerships: The State of the Art." October 16, 1985. *Education Week.*

Seminole County School Board & Seminole Community College. 1986. *Agreements for the Admission of Students for Accelerated Programs (Dual Enrollment).* Sanford, Fla.

Sexton, P.C. 1961. *Education and Income.* New York: Viking Press.

Shaffer, E.C., and W.C. Bryant. 1983. *Structures and Processes for Effective Collaboration among Local Schools, Colleges, and Universities: A Collective Project of Annapolis City Schools.* Charlotte, N.C.: Livingstone College, University of North Carolina-Charlotte.

Shapiro, B.C. 1986. "Two Plus Two: The High School/Community College Connection." *National Association of Secondary School Principals Bulletin,* (70)494. EJ 345 306.

Sizer, T.R. 1984. *Horace's Compromise: The Dilemma of the American High School.* Boston: Houghton-Mifflin.

———. Not dated. *The Coalition of Essential Schools.* Providence, R.I.: Brown University Education Department.

Smith, M.P. 1985. "Early Identification and Support: The University of California-Berkeley's MESA Program." In *College-School Collaboration: Appraising the Major Approaches,* edited by W. T. Daly, 19–25. New Directions for Teaching and Learning No. 24. San Francisco: Jossey-Bass.

Snyder, N.C. October 1974. "School*college [sic] Articulation and the Maginot Line." Paper presented at Commissioner's Second Annual Conference on Nontraditional Studies. Glens Falls, N.Y.

Sosniak, L.A. 1988. *Partnerships with a Purpose: A Report on Two Programs for Curriculum Development and Delivery,* within the Educational EQuality Project's Models Program for School-College

Collaboration. New York: The College Board.

Spurr, S.F. 1970. "Secondary Schools-University Articulation." In *Academic Degree Structures: Innovative Approaches*. New York: McGraw-Hill.

Stanfield, R.L. 1981. "Teamwork for High Schools and Colleges." *Educational Record*, 62(2).

Stoel, C.F. 1988. "History of the High School Connection." In *Collaborating with High Schools*, edited by J.E. Lieberman, 13–23. New Directions for Community Colleges, No. 63. San Francisco: Jossey-Bass.

Suss, S., and R. Goldsmith. 1989. "College Now Program: Successful Transition for Moderate Achievers." *College Teaching* (37)2.

Sutherland, A.R., R. Leonard, G.D. Edwards, and J.R. Hutto. April 1990. "Statewide Articulation Cannot be Done Tongue In Cheek." *Leadership Abstracts*. Austin: University of Texas.

Thomson, S.D. 1984. "School-College Connection." In *The School-College Connection: Relationships and Standards*. Reston, Va.: National Association of Secondary School Principals.

Townsend, F. 1980. *Beginning and Administering an Advanced Placement Program in a Secondary School*. New York: College Entrance Examination Board.

Tyler, J.L., D. Gruber, and B.J. McMullan. September 1987. "An Evaluation of the City University of New York/New York City Board of Education Collaborative Programs." Mimeographed. Philadelphia: Public/Private Ventures.

Van de Walter, G. 1988. "The Governance of School-College Collaboratives: Lessons Learned from the College Board's Educational EQuality Project Models Program for School-College Collaboration." Draft. New York: The College Board.

Van Gelder, E. 1972. *The Three-Year B.A.: A Wavering Idea*. Gainesville: Florida University. ED O70 434.

Vivian, J.R. 1985a. "The Concept of the Yale-New Haven Teachers Institute: The Primacy of Teachers." In *Teaching in America: The Common Ground, A Report of the Yale-New Haven Teachers Institute*. New York: The College Board.

———. 1985b. "Empowering Teachers as Colleagues: The Yale-New Haven Teachers Institute." In *College-School Collaboration: Appraising the Major Approaches*, edited by W.T. Daly, 79–89. New Directions for Teaching and Learning No. 24. San Francisco: Jossey-Bass.

Watkins, B.T. 16 February 1983. "Cooperation Said to be Increasing between High Schools, Colleges." *Chronicle of Higher Education*: 25(23).

Wilbur, F.P. 1984. "School-College Partnerships: Building Effective Models for Collaboration." In *The school-College Connection: Relationships and Standards*. Reston, Va.: National Association of Secondary School Principals.

Wilbur, F.P., and J.W. LaFay. Fall 1978. "The Transferability of College

Credit Earned During High School: An Update." *College and University*. 54(1).

Wilbur, F.P., L.M. Lambert, and M.J. Young. 1987. *National Directory of School-College Partnerships: Current Models and Practices*. Washington, D.C.: American Association for Higher Education. ED 295 514. MF–01; PC–06.

Wimmer, D.K. 1988. "Enabling Professionalism: The Master Technician Program." In *Collaborating with High Schools*, edited by J.E. Lieberman, 95–100. New Directions for Community Colleges No. 63. San Francisco: Jossey-Bass.

Yount, R., and N. Magrun. 1989. *School/College Collaboration: Teaching At-Risk Youth*. Washington, D.C.: Council of Chief State School Officers.

INDEX

High school principals
    duties, 22
    leadership roles, 22
High-School College Partnerships, 1
Holmes Group, 71

I

Institutional funding, 17

J

Johns Hopkins University
    CTY, 56
Johns Hopkins University three-year collegiate program, 9
Joint curriculum planning, 29

K

Kenmore High School/Akron University of, 74
    writing project, 74
Kenyon Plan, 10
Kingsborough Community College
    College Now Program, 37

L

LaGuardia Community College
    concurrent enrollment,17
    Middle College High School, 43
Leadership processes, 22
Liberty Partnerships Program, 2
Local reform partnerships, 75
Los Angeles Unified School District
    Dropout Prevention and Retention program, 78

M

MacArthur Foundation, 2, 62
Massachusetts University of, Boston, 63
Massachusetts Office of Economic Affairs, 76
Mathematics, Engineering, Science Achievement (MESA)
    Program, 54
Mentoring/tutoring programs, 72
Miami-Dade Community College
    Partners in Education Program, 57
Michigan University of, 8
Middle States Association, 8
Middle College, 1, 2, 43
    admissions, 44
    curriculum, 44
    high school, 17
    limitations, 45

Student population, 4
 colleges, 18
 high schools, 18
Student acceleration, 10
Syracuse University
 College Now, 1
 Project Advance, 1, 34

T

Teacher Training Centers, 72
Teacher-to-Teacher partnerships, 59, 61, 62
Teachers and teaching
 accreditation, 21
 certification, 21
 colleges, 19
 dialogues, 64
 high schools, 19
 licensing, 21
Teachers Institute
 Yale-New Haven, 68
Two Plus Two Programs, 43

U

Urban Initiative Language Education Program, 64

V

Virginia
 Master Technician Program, 46
 State Board of Education, 46

Y

Yale-New Haven Teachers Institute, 68
 evaluation, 69

ASHE-ERIC HIGHER EDUCATION REPORTS

Since 1983, the Association for the Study of Higher Education (ASHE) and the Educational Resources Information Center (ERIC) Clearinghouse on Higher Education, a sponsored project of the School of Education and Human Development at The George Washington University, have cosponsored the *ASHE-ERIC Higher Education Report* series. The 1991 series is the twentieth overall and the third to be published by the School of Education and Human Development at the George Washington University.

Each monograph is the definitive analysis of a tough higher education problem, based on thorough research of pertinent literature and institutional experiences. Topics are identified by a national survey. Noted practitioners and scholars are then commissioned to write the reports, with experts providing critical reviews of each manuscript before publication.

Eight monographs (10 before 1985) in the ASHE-ERIC Higher Education Report series are published each year and are available on individual and subscription bases. Subscription to eight issues is $90.00 annually; $70 to members of AAHE, AIR, or AERA; and $60 to ASHE members. All foreign subscribers must include an additional $10 per series year for postage.

To order single copies of existing reports, use the order form on the last page of this book. Regular prices, and special rates available to members of AAHE, AIR, AERA and ASHE, are as follows:

Series	Regular	Members
1990 and 91	$17.00	$12.75
1988 and 89	15.00	11.25
1985 to 87	10.00	7.50
1983 and 84	7.50	6.00
before 1983	6.50	5.00

Price includes book rate postage within the U.S. For foreign orders, please add $1.00 per book. Fast United Parcel Service available within the contiguous U.S. at $2.50 for each order under $50.00, and calculated at 5% of invoice total for orders $50.00 or above.

All orders under $45.00 must be prepaid. Make check payable to ASHE-ERIC. For Visa or MasterCard, include card number, expiration date and signature. A bulk discount of 10% is available on orders of 10 or more books, and 40% on orders of 25 or more books (not applicable on subscriptions).

Address order to
ASHE-ERIC Higher Education Reports
The George Washington University
1 Dupont Circle, Suite 630
Washington, DC 20036
Or phone (202) 296-2597
Write or call for a complete catalog.

1991 ASHE-ERIC Higher Education Reports

1. Active Learning: Creating Excitement in the Classroom
   Charles C. Bonwell and James A. Eison

2. Realizing Gender Equality in Higher Education: The Need to Integrate Work/Family Issues
   Nancy Hensel

3. Academic Advising for Student Success: A System of Shared Responsibility
   by Susan H. Frost

4. Cooperative Learning: Increasing College Faculty Instructional Productivity
   by David W. Johnson, Roger T. Johnson, and Karl A. Smith

1990 ASHE-ERIC Higher Education Reports

1. The Campus Green: Fund Raising in Higher Education
   Barbara E. Brittingham and Thomas R. Pezzullo

2. The Emeritus Professor: Old Rank - New Meaning
   James E. Mauch, Jack W. Birch, and Jack Matthews

3. "High Risk" Students in Higher Education: Future Trends
   Dionne J. Jones and Betty Collier Watson

4. Budgeting for Higher Education at the State Level: Enigma, Paradox, and Ritual
   Daniel T. Layzell and Jan W. Lyddon

5. Proprietary Schools: Programs, Policies, and Prospects
   John B. Lee and Jamie P. Merisotis

6. College Choice: Understanding Student Enrollment Behavior
   Michael B. Paulsen

7. Pursuing Diversity: Recruiting College Minority Students
   Barbara Astone and Elsa Nuñez-Wormack

8. Social Consciousness and Career Awareness: Emerging Link in Higher Education
   John S. Swift, Jr.

1989 ASHE-ERIC Higher Education Reports

1. Making Sense of Administrative Leadership: The 'L' Word in Higher Education
   Estela M. Bensimon, Anna Neumann, and Robert Birnbaum

2. Affirmative Rhetoric, Negative Action: African-American and Hispanic Faculty at Predominantly White Universities
   Valora Washington and William Harvey

3. Postsecondary Developmental Programs: A Traditional Agenda with New Imperatives
   Louise M. Tomlinson

4. The Old College Try: Balancing Athletics and Academics in Higher Education
   John R. Thelin and Lawrence L. Wiseman

5. The Challenge of Diversity: Involvement or Alienation in the Academy?
   Daryl G. Smith

6. Student Goals for College and Courses: A Missing Link in Assessing and Improving Academic Achievement
   Joan S. Stark, Kathleen M. Shaw, and Malcolm A. Lowther

7. The Student as Commuter: Developing a Comprehensive Institutional Response
   Barbara Jacoby

8. Renewing Civic Capacity: Preparing College Students for Service and Citizenship
   Suzanne W. Morse

1988 ASHE-ERIC Higher Education Reports

1. The Invisible Tapestry: Culture in American Colleges and Universities
   George D. Kuh and Elizabeth J. Whitt

2. Critical Thinking: Theory, Research, Practice, and Possibilities
   Joanne Gainen Kurfiss

3. Developing Academic Programs: The Climate for Innovation
   Daniel T. Seymour

4. Peer Teaching: To Teach is To Learn Twice
   Neal A. Whitman

5. Higher Education and State Governments: Renewed Partnership, Cooperation, or Competition?
   Edward R. Hines

6. Entrepreneurship and Higher Education: Lessons for Colleges, Universities, and Industry
   James S. Fairweather

7. Planning for Microcomputers in Higher Education: Strategies for the Next Generation
   Reynolds Ferrante, John Hayman, Mary Susan Carlson, and Harry Phillips

8. The Challenge for Research in Higher Education: Harmonizing Excellence and Utility
   Alan W. Lindsay and Ruth T. Neumann

1987 ASHE-ERIC Higher Education Reports

1. Incentive Early Retirement Programs for Faculty: Innovative Responses to a Changing Environment
   Jay L. Chronister and Thomas R. Kepple, Jr.

2. Working Effectively with Trustees: Building Cooperative Campus Leadership
   Barbara E. Taylor

3. Formal Recognition of Employer-Sponsored Instruction: Conflict and Collegiality in Postsecondary Education
   Nancy S. Nash and Elizabeth M. Hawthorne

4. Learning Styles: Implications for Improving Educational Practices
   Charles S. Claxton and Patricia H. Murrell

5. Higher Education Leadership: Enhancing Skills through Professional Development Programs
   Sharon A. McDade

6. Higher Education and the Public Trust: Improving Stature in Colleges and Universities
   Richard L. Alfred and Julie Weissman

7. College Student Outcomes Assessment: A Talent Development Perspective
   Maryann Jacobi, Alexander Astin, and Frank Ayala, Jr.

8. Opportunity from Strength: Strategic Planning Clarified with Case Examples
   Robert G. Cope

1986 ASHE-ERIC Higher Education Reports

1. Post-tenure Faculty Evaluation: Threat or Opportunity?
   Christine M. Licata

2. Blue Ribbon Commissions and Higher Education: Changing Academe from the Outside
   Janet R. Johnson and Laurence R. Marcus

3. Responsive Professional Education: Balancing Outcomes and Opportunities
   Joan S. Stark, Malcolm A. Lowther, and Bonnie M.K. Hagerty

4. Increasing Students' Learning: A Faculty Guide to Reducing Stress among Students
   Neal A. Whitman, David C. Spendlove, and Claire H. Clark

5. Student Financial Aid and Women: Equity Dilemma?
   Mary Moran

6. The Master's Degree: Tradition, Diversity, Innovation
   Judith S. Glazer

7. The College, the Constitution, and the Consumer Student: Implications for Policy and Practice
   Robert M. Hendrickson and Annette Gibbs

8. Selecting College and University Personnel: The Quest and the Question
   Richard A. Kaplowitz

1985 ASHE-ERIC Higher Education Reports

1. Flexibility in Academic Staffing: Effective Policies and Practices
   Kenneth P. Mortimer, Marque Bagshaw, and Andrew T. Masland

2. Associations in Action: The Washington, D.C. Higher Education Community
   Harland G. Bloland

3. And on the Seventh Day: Faculty Consulting and Supplemental Income
   Carol M. Boyer and Darrell R. Lewis

4. Faculty Research Performance: Lessons from the Sciences and Social Sciences
   John W. Creswell

5. Academic Program Review: Institutional Approaches, Expectations, and Controversies
   Clifton F. Conrad and Richard F. Wilson

6. Students in Urban Settings: Achieving the Baccalaureate Degree
   Richard C. Richardson, Jr. and Louis W. Bender

7. Serving More Than Students: A Critical Need for College Student Personnel Services
   Peter H. Garland

8. Faculty Participation in Decision Making: Necessity or Luxury?
   Carol E. Floyd

1984 ASHE-ERIC Higher Education Reports

1. Adult Learning: State Policies and Institutional Practices
   K. Patricia Cross and Anne-Marie McCartan

2. Student Stress: Effects and Solutions
   Neal A. Whitman, David C. Spendlove, and Claire H. Clark

3. Part-time Faulty: Higher Education at a Crossroads
   Judith M. Gappa

4. Sex Discrimination Law in Higher Education: The Lessons of the Past Decade. ED 252 169.*
   J. Ralph Lindgren, Patti T. Ota, Perry A. Zirkel, and Nan Van Gieson

5. Faculty Freedoms and Institutional Accountability: Interactions and Conflicts
   Steven G. Olswang and Barbara A. Lee

6. The High Technology Connection: Academic/Industrial Cooperation for Economic Growth
   Lynn G. Johnson

7. Employee Educational Programs: Implications for Industry and Higher Education. ED 258 501.*
   Suzanne W. Morse

8. Academic Libraries: The Changing Knowledge Centers of Colleges and Universities
   Barbara B. Moran

9. Futures Research and the Strategic Planning Process: Implications for Higher Education
   James L. Morrison, William L. Renfro, and Wayne I. Boucher

10. Faculty Workload: Research, Theory, and Interpretation
    Harold E. Yuker

1983 ASHE-ERIC Higher Education Reports

1. The Path to Excellence: Quality Assurance in Higher Education
   Laurence R. Marcus, Anita O. Leone, and Edward D. Goldberg

2. Faculty Recruitment, Retention, and Fair Employment: Obligations and Opportunities
   John S. Waggaman

3. Meeting the Challenges: Developing Faculty Careers. ED 232 516.*
   Michael C.T. Brooks and Katherine L. German

4. Raising Academic Standards: A Guide to Learning Improvement
   Ruth Talbott Keimig

5. Serving Learners at a Distance: A Guide to Program Practices
   Charles E. Feasley

6. Competence, Admissions, and Articulation: Returning to the Basics in Higher Education
   Jean L. Preer

7. Public Service in Higher Education: Practices and Priorities
   Patricia H. Crosson

8. Academic Employment and Retrenchment: Judicial Review and Administrative Action
   Robert M. Hendrickson and Barbara A. Lee

9. Burnout: The New Academic Disease. ED 242 255.*
   Winifred Albizu Meléndez and Rafael M. de Guzmán

10. Academic Workplace: New Demands, Heightened Tensions
    Ann E. Austin and Zelda F. Gamson

*Out-of-print. Available through EDRS. Call 1-800-443-ERIC.

ORDER FORM

Quantity   **Amount**

_____ Please begin my subscription to the 1991 *ASHE-ERIC Higher Education Reports* at $90.00, 33% off the cover price, starting with Report 1, 1991.   _____

_____ Please send a complete set of the 1990 *ASHE-ERIC Higher Education Reports* at $80.00, 41% off the cover price.   _____

_____ Outside the U.S., add $10.00 per series for postage.   _____

Individual reports are avilable at the following prices:

1990 and 1991, $17.00	1983 and 1984, $7.50
1988 and 1989, $15.00	1982 and back, $6.50
1985 to 1987, $10.00	

Book rate postage within the U.S. is included. Outside U.S., please add $1.00 per book for postage. Fast U.P.S. shipping is available within the contiguous U.S. at $2.50 for each order under $50.00, and calculated at 5% of invoice total for orders $50.00 or above. All orders under $45.00 must be prepaid.

PLEASE SEND ME THE FOLLOWING REPORTS:

Quantity	Report No.	Year	Title	Amount

Subtotal:	
Foreign or UPS:	
Total Due:	

Please check one of the following:
- ☐ Check enclosed, payable to GWU–ERIC.
- ☐ Purchase order attached ($45.00 minimum).
- ☐ Charge my credit card indicated below:
  - ☐ Visa   ☐ MasterCard

Expiration Date _____

Name _____

Title _____

Institution _____

Address _____

City _____ State _____ Zip _____

Phone _____

Signature _____ Date _____

SEND ALL ORDERS TO:
ASHE-ERIC Higher Education Reports
The George Washington University
One Dupont Circle, Suite 630
Washington, DC 20036-1183
Phone: (202) 296-2597